Relational Attribute Blocks Activity Book

Grades 1-6

Barbara Bando Irvin

Table of Contents

Introduction

Relational Attribute Blocks engages children in exploring basic math concepts and learning problem-solving strategies. Designed for grades 1-6, the set of manipulatives consists of 60 durable plastic pieces in four attributes – shape, color, size, and thickness – and five shapes – square, rectangle, triangle, circle, and hexagon. The two sizes are large and small, and the two thicknesses are thick and thin.

Children may use everyday language to describe a specific block. Encourage students to use the correct terms: *square, triangle, circle, rectangle,* and *hexagon.* However, use your judgment when correcting children because it is more important for them to understand a concept in their own words, rather than a vocabulary word or phrase. Gradually children will use the correct math terms when discussing the relational attribute blocks.

This activity book contains eight sections:

- Learning About Shapes
- Shape Puzzles
- More Shape Puzzles
- Attribute Differences
- Logic Problems
- Making Arrangements
- Shapes and Fractions
- Perimeter and Area

Activities build on students' prior knowledge to ensure a logical progression of skill development. It is easy to weave math topics into your math curriculum for grades 1-6.

Topics covered in this book include the following:

- Shapes
- Matching
- Sorting
- Comparing
- Counting
- Whole Numbers
- Fractions
- Logic and Reasoning
- Geometric Shapes
- Geometric Relationships
- Permutations
- Problem Solving
- Measuring
- Perimeter and Area

Using This Book

In addition to the activity-based, reproducible blackline masters, *Teaching Notes* are included at the beginning of each section. Suggestions are provided in sections entitled *Warm Up, Using the Activity Pages,* and *Wrap Up.* Objectives and vocabulary are included to help you plan your lessons.

In the section entitled *Solutions,* pages 87-92, you will find answers to most problems, including those with several possible answers.

Use the section entitled *Relational Attribute Block Relationships,* page 93, as a reference page. Make copies and distribute to students.

See the section entitled *Relational Attribute Block Dimensions,* page 94, for the actual dimensions of the blocks.

Use the *Family-Gram,* the *Good Work Certificate,* and the *Award Certificate* on the last two pages of this book. The *Family-Gram* can be addressed to the child or the child's family to make special note of progress or for take-home reminders. Use the *Good Work Certificate* and the *Award Certificate* to praise children on their improved work habits, social skills, and academic accomplishments.

Children can work individually, in pairs, or in small groups depending on the lesson. Use the activities as part of a specific math lesson or in a learning center where children can work independently.

Encourage children to share their discoveries and solutions with their classmates. From time to time, suggest that students write about their ideas by completing a sentence or story, making a picture or story book, or creating challenging puzzles to share with each other.

Duplicate the blackline masters, and give each child a set of blocks. Make extra copies of blackline masters for activities that have several solutions. Children can then record their solutions by tracing, coloring, or writing directly on the activity pages.

NCTM Standards

Curriculum and Evaluation Standards for School Mathematics, published by the National Council of Teachers of Mathematics (NCTM), was used as a guide in preparing this book. Special attention was paid to *Standard 9: Geometry and Spatial Sense,* which suggests that the math curriculum include these goals for children in grades K-4:

- Describe, model, draw, and classify shapes.
- Investigate and predict the results of combining, subdividing, and changing shapes.
- Develop spatial sense.
- Relate geometric ideas to number and measurement ideas.
- Recognize and appreciate geometry in the world.

Making a Set of Relational Attribute Blocks

Each child needs a set of relational attribute blocks. Duplicate three copies of page 7 for each child. Have children color each page, one with red, one with blue, and one with yellow blocks. Then direct them to cut apart the blocks. Or duplicate page 7 on red, blue, and yellow paper, and have each child cut out the blocks from each of the three colored pages.

To make thick blocks, cut out shapes on paper and cardboard or corrugated boxes. Glue paper shapes onto matching box shapes.

Each child then should have a 60-piece set of paper blocks that matches Learning Resources' set of 60 plastic relational attribute blocks. Provide large envelopes or plastic Ziploc bags for children to store their blocks.

Exploring the Blocks

Allow at least one class period for children to explore the relational attribute blocks on their own. Permitting children to freely explore with the blocks fulfills two objectives: 1) students become familiar with the blocks and begin to think about the shapes and their relationships; and 2) you gain insight into children's thinking to help guide your instruction.

Observe children as they work with the blocks, and listen to their conversations. One child may sort blocks by shape, another child may stack them, while still another may form a colorful design. Compliment children on their discoveries, and encourage them to look for more attributes and relationships.

Sorting the Blocks

Determine what children already know about the shapes. Some children may wish to sort the blocks into smaller groups using two or three attributes, such as "small circles," "thick squares," or "large thin hexagons." Prior to sorting, these activities prepare children to easily find and manipulate the relational attribute blocks.

Schedule a few class periods for children to sort the blocks by attribute. Begin with color. Be sure children can identify *red*, *blue*, and *yellow*. Then sort the blocks by size — *large* and *small*; and by thickness — *thick* and *thin*. Finally, sort by *shape*.

Relational Attribute Blocks

Section A: Learning About Shapes
Teaching Notes

Activities in this section help children to become familiar with the relational attribute blocks. These activities also encourage the use of descriptive vocabulary when referring to the blocks. Initially children may talk about a "red fat box" to describe a "red thick rectangle (or square)." Gradually reinforce the use of the descriptive vocabulary.

Objectives

● Identify the blocks by shape, color, size, and thickness.
● Describe a block by its attributes.
● Count the number of blocks.

Vocabulary

Shapes: *square, triangle, circle, rectangle, hexagon*
Colors: *red, blue, yellow*
Sizes: *large, small*
Thicknesses: *thick, thin*

Warm-Up

Ask children to point out red, blue, and yellow items of clothing or objects in the classroom. Ask about large and small, as well as thick and thin objects. Encourage them to identify objects that are "round" (curved, oval) and those with "corners" such as a box or a door.

When using the activity pages, children need to know that the letters *R, B,* and *Y* designate the colors *red, blue,* and *yellow.* Also, the *thin* and *thick* outlines of the shapes designate thickness. You can write this information on a blackboard as a reminder.

Using the Activity Pages

Square *(page 10)*

Introduce the *square* by displaying all the square shapes. Then show a few differently shaped blocks. Ask students to explain how the square is different (four sides of equal length). Tell them to find objects in the classroom that are shaped like squares.

Distribute copies of page 10 to children. Have them cover each shape with all blocks that match. Then have them color the shapes to record their answers. Ask which three squares are not used (large thick red square, large thick blue square, large thin yellow square). Also ask how many squares on the activity page are large (3), small (6), thick (4), thin (5), red (3), blue (3), and yellow (3).

Relational Attribute Blocks
© 1993 Learning Resources, Inc.

Older children could describe the square more technically — a quadrilateral with equivalent sides and right (90°) angles.

▲riangle *(page 11)*

For the *triangle,* adapt the activity you used for the square on page 10. Ask the following: How does a triangle differ from a square? Are any triangles left over? (No.) Then tell students to count the number of triangles that are small (6), large (6), thick (6), thin (6), red (4), blue (4), and yellow (4). You might point out that the right side of the figure is a reflection of the left side.

Older children may describe this triangle as an equilateral shape with 60° angles.

●ircle *(page 12)*

Separate the *circle* blocks and adapt the activity for the square on page 10. Ask children which circular blocks are left over after they complete the activity page (large blue thick circle; large thin yellow circle; small thin blue circle). Have children count the number of circles on the activity page that are large (4), small (5), thick (5), thin (4), red (4), blue (2), yellow (3). Also ask if there are more small circles than large or as many blue circles as red.

Ask older children to measure the diameter of the two circles (3 inches, 1½ inches), and then determine their radii. (The radius is half of the diameter: 1½ inches, ¾ inch.)

▮ectangle *(page 13)*

Introduce the *rectangle* to children using the rectangular blocks. Adapt the activity for the square on page 10. Ask children how squares and rectangles are the same and how they are different. Encourage children to explore the relationships between the large and small rectangles (see Relational Attribute Block Relationships, page 93).

⬡exagon *(page 14)*

Using the *hexagon* blocks, repeat the activity for the square on page 10. Showing the children a set of squares, rectangles, triangles, and hexagons, ask which shapes have the most and fewest number of sides. Ask children which hexagon block is left over after the figure is completed (large thin red hexagon). Have children count the number of large (5), small (6), thick (6), thin (5), red (3), blue (4), and yellow (4) blocks shown on the activity page. Also ask if there are more or fewer large blocks than small.

Ask older children the size of the interior angles of the hexagon (120°). Ask them how they can determine the angle measure without using a protractor. (Answer: Two small triangles, each with 60° angles, can fit into the interior angle of a large hexagon, which is 120°).

Wrap-Up

Place four or five relational attribute blocks in a cloth bag or a paper sack. Ask the child to choose a block and then describe it.

Extension Activity

Children can create their own figures or designs using some or all of the relational attribute blocks. Provide large paper for tracing and coloring the blocks. Then ask them to describe their drawings to classmates. Display them on the classroom bulletin board.

Square

Name _____

➤ Cover the shapes with the blocks, and show the teacher.

➤ Color the shapes you covered.

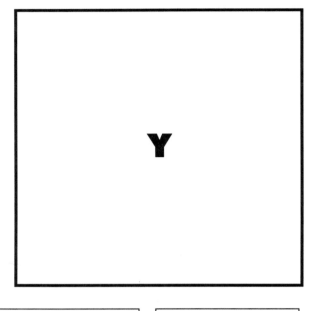

Y

B

Y

R

Use **THICK** and THIN blocks.

R

B

Y

B

R

Triangle

Name _____

➤ Cover the shapes with the blocks, and show the teacher.

➤ Color the shapes you covered.

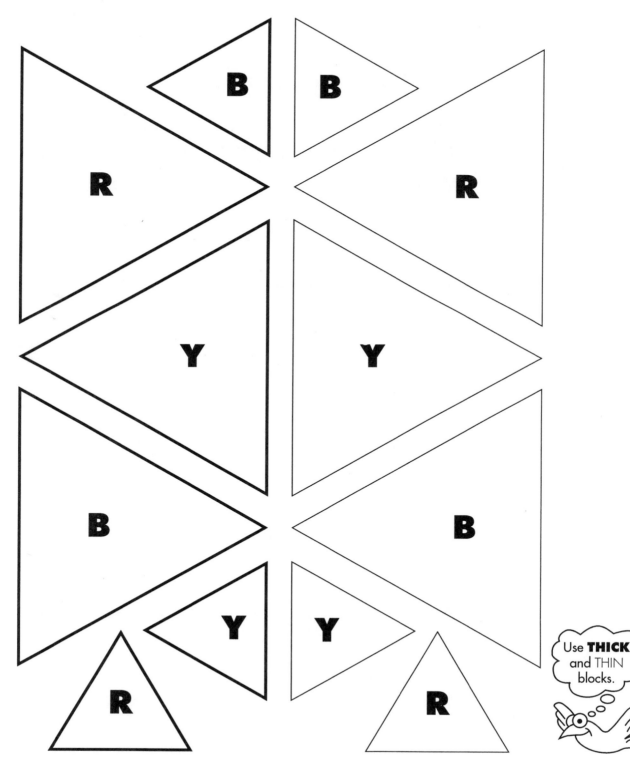

Use **THICK** and THIN blocks.

Circle

Name _____

➤ Cover the shapes with the blocks, and show the teacher.
➤ Color the shapes you covered.

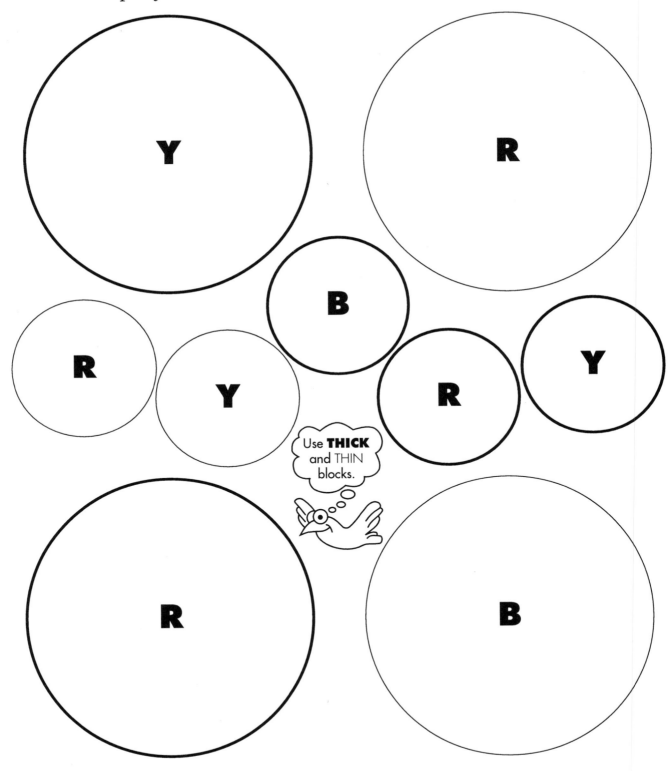

Relational Attribute Blocks
© 1993 Learning Resources, Inc.

Rectangle

Name _____

➤ Cover the shapes with the blocks, and show the teacher.

➤ Color the shapes you covered.

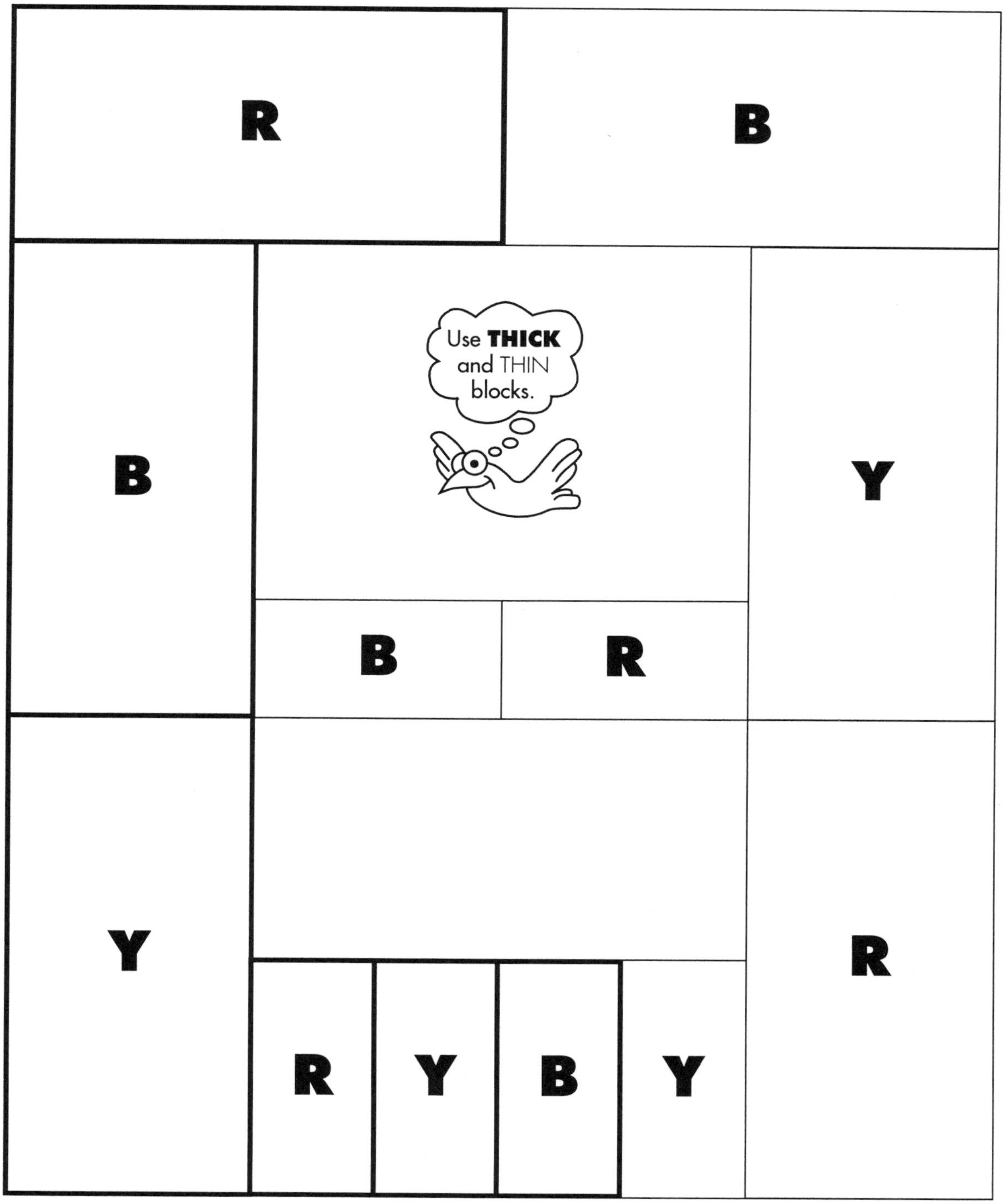

R

B

B

Use **THICK** and THIN blocks.

Y

B   R

Y

R

R   Y   B   Y

Hexagon

Name _____

➤ Cover the shapes with the blocks, and show the teacher.

➤ Color the shapes you covered.

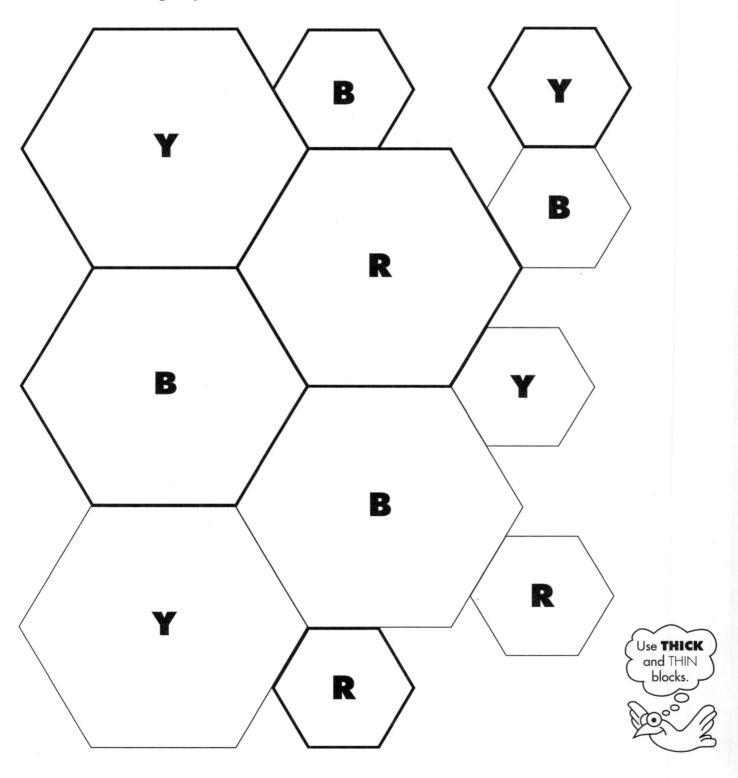

Use **THICK** and THIN blocks.

Section B: Shape Puzzles
Teaching Notes

In this section, children form shapes with and without inside lines. These activities help children sharpen their shape recognition and perceptual skills.

The activities on pages 23, 24, and 25 are more challenging because students must figure out which blocks to use and keep a record of solutions on the charts.

Objectives

Make a shape by:
- placing blocks on pictures of blocks;
- matching blocks;
- placing blocks within an outline.

Vocabulary

Shape, outline, model

Warm-Up

Pair up children to play the "Copy Cat" game. Direct one child to

make a shape using three or four blocks. Then encourage the other child to model, or recreate, the shape using his or her own blocks. Repeat the activity several times.

Using the Activity Pages

House *(page 17)*

On page 17, children match the blocks to the outlines shown in the "House." Give students a hint by explaining that some blocks are placed on top of each other. Ask them how many and which blocks are used to make the house picture. *Note:* 11 blocks are used in all: small thick yellow circle for the sun, small thick blue rectangle for the door, and so on.

Circus Truck *(page 18)*

Direct children to match the blocks to the outlines shown in the "Circus Truck" on page 18. Ask children how many blocks are used in all (13). Then ask how many blocks are large (3), small (10), red (2), blue (6), yellow (5), thick (8), and thin (5).

Robot *(page 19)*

Challenge students to form the robot shape with their blocks. Have children take turns describing the blocks and how many they use (15). Display the robot pictures in the classroom.

Dog *(page 20)*

To make dogs, children can match blocks to the outlines on page 20. Notice that the color designations *R*, *B*, and *Y* have been omitted, and the outlines of the blocks are drawn with dashed lines, so children can make their own block arrangements. Ask children to take turns describing the blocks and how many they used to make the dog (11). Display their pictures in the classroom.

Block Bear *(page 21)*

This activity is similar to the "Dog" on page 20. Ask children about the number (17) and types of blocks they use to complete the picture. Ask if they can make the block bear with fewer than 17 blocks. *Hint:* The body can be replaced by a large square, two large rectangles, or one large rectangle and two small squares to total 14, 15, or 16 blocks, respectively. Replacing the body with four small squares would still use a total of 17 blocks.

Next, ask children if they can make the block bear using more than 17 blocks. *Hint:* The body can contain three small squares and two small rectangles for 18 blocks; two small squares and four small rectangles for 19 blocks.

School *(page 22)*

Direct children to make the school building shown. Notice that the color designations *R*, *B*, and *Y* have been omitted, and the outlines of the blocks are drawn with dashed lines, so children can create their own designs. Have children take turns describing the blocks and how many they use (15). Display their pictures.

Fill the Square *(page 23)*

Children complete the chart to show all seven possible ways to fill the square. For an added activity, ask children to show as many possible color combinations for the square as they can.

Fill the Shape *(page 24)*

Children need to figure out which blocks will fill in the outline of the shape. Since there are several solutions, have children keep track of their answers by completing the chart at the top of the activity page. Ask children if they know the name of this shape (trapezoid).

Fill It Up! *(page 25)*

Ask children if they can name the type of polygon shown on page 25 (hexagon). Then have them find all eight solutions to the problem and record them on the chart. *Note:* There are two ways to form this shape using six blocks.

Wrap-Up

Draw an outline of two large squares to form a rectangle. Encourage children to find all the ways to fill this outline with the blocks.

House

Name _____

➤ Cover the shapes with blocks, and show the teacher.

➤ Color the house.

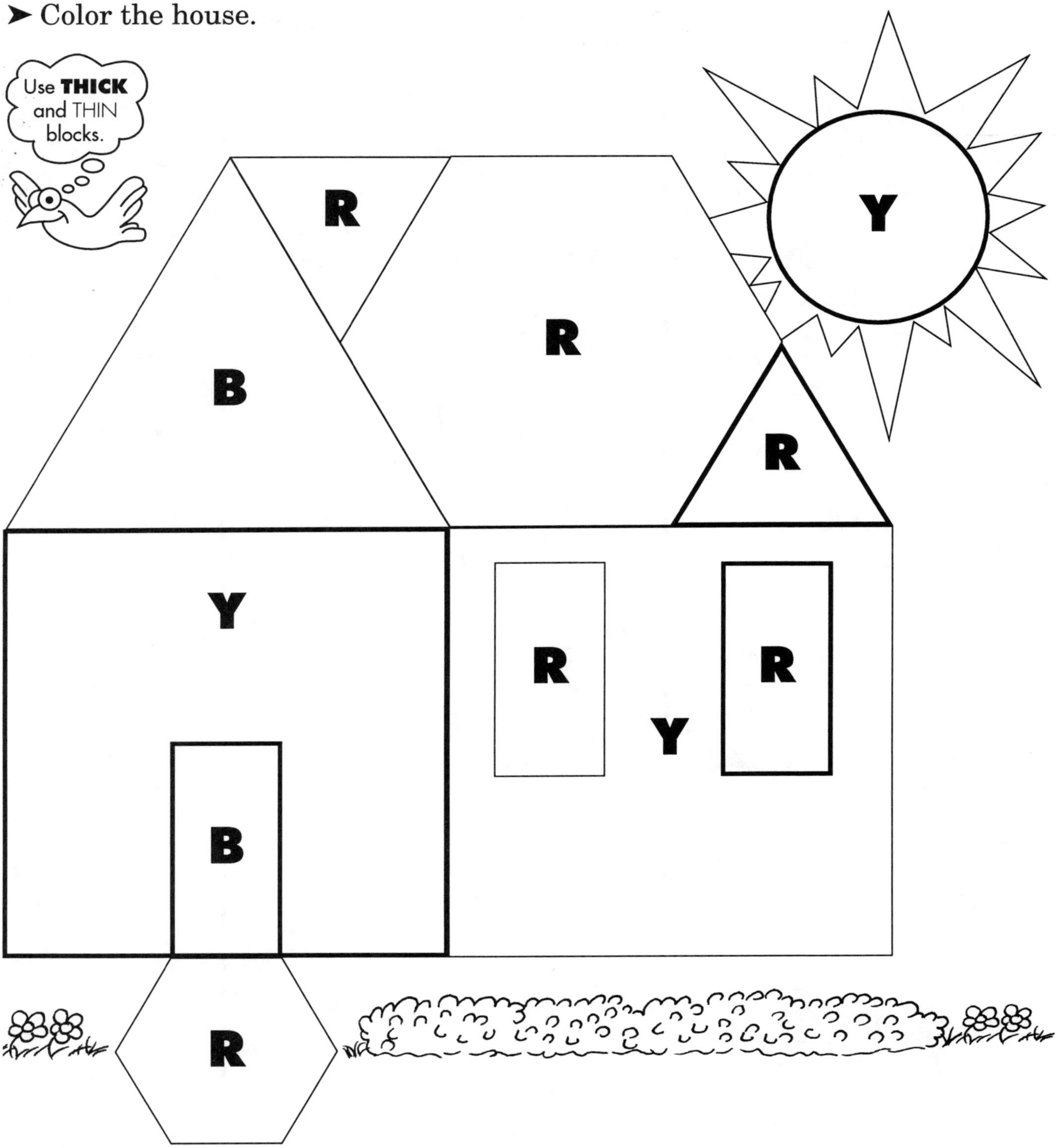

Use **THICK** and THIN blocks.

R

R

Y

B

R

Y

B

R

R

Y

R

Circus Truck

Name_____

➤ Cover the shapes with the blocks, and show the teacher.

➤ Color the truck.

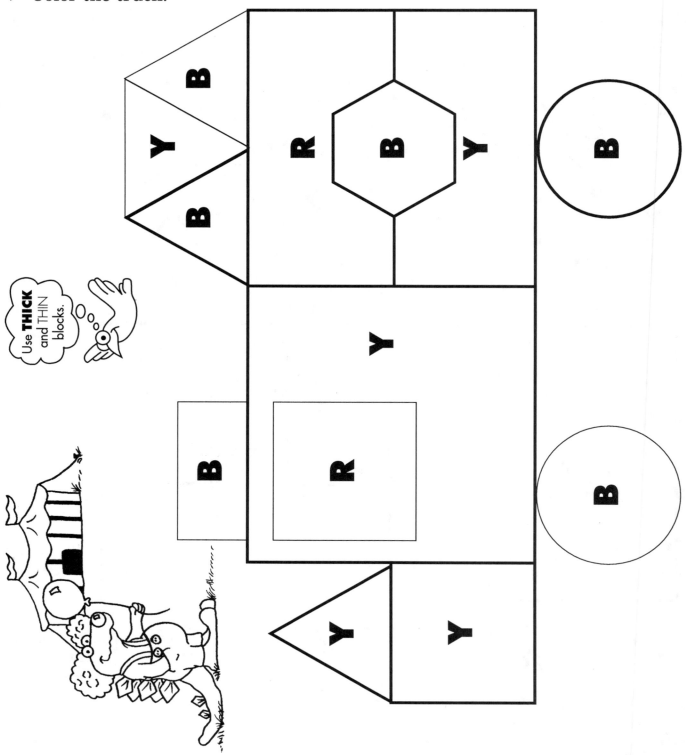

Use **THICK** and THIN blocks.

Relational Attribute Blocks
© 1993 Learning Resources, Inc.

Robot

Name _____

➤ Make a robot with blocks, and show the teacher.

➤ Color the robot.

Use **THICK** and THIN blocks.

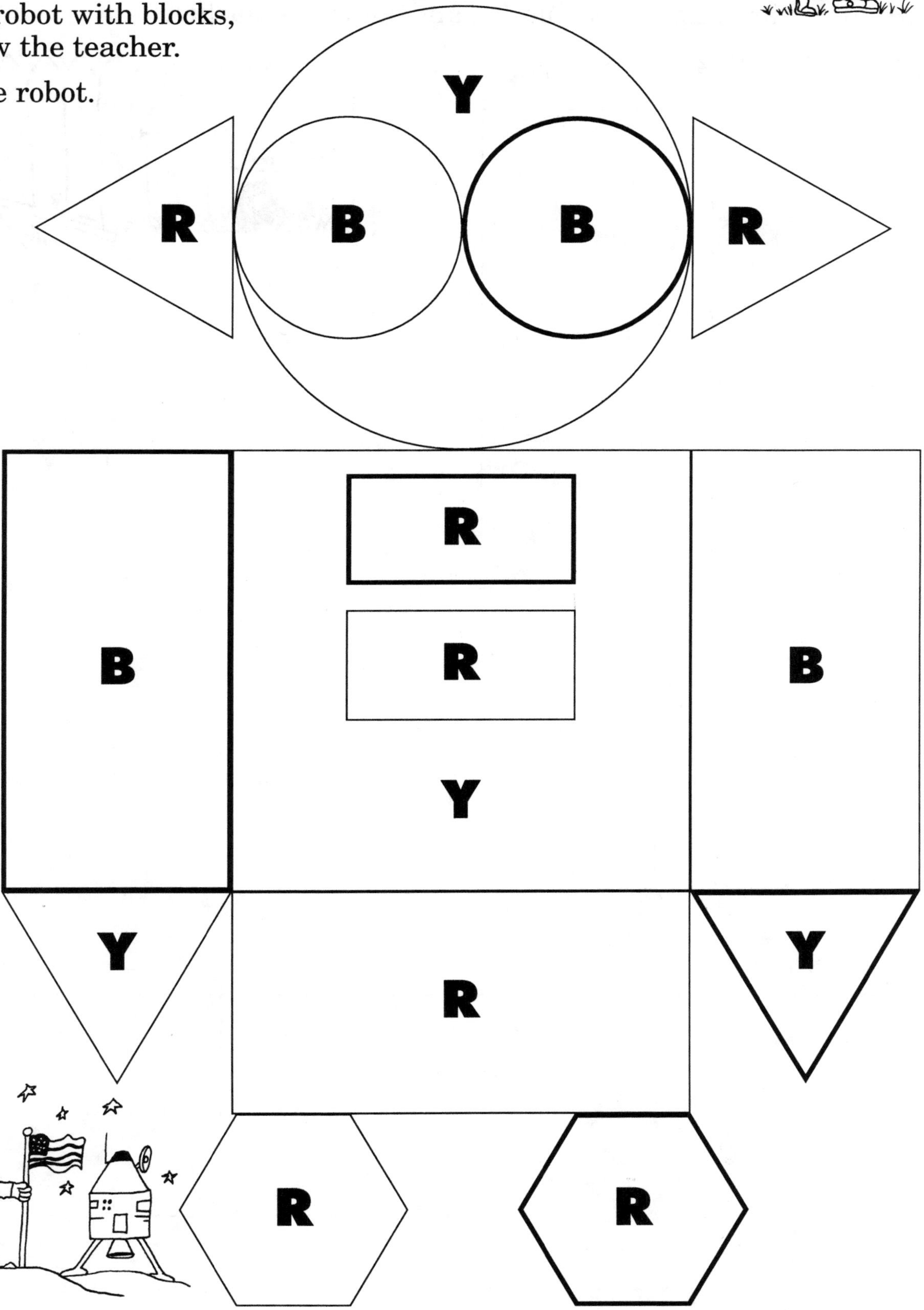

Y

R

B

B

R

B

R

R

Y

B

Y

R

Y

R

R

Dog

Name _____

➤ Cover the shapes with blocks, and show the teacher.

➤ Color the dog.

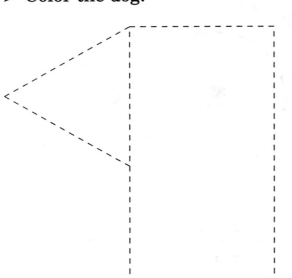

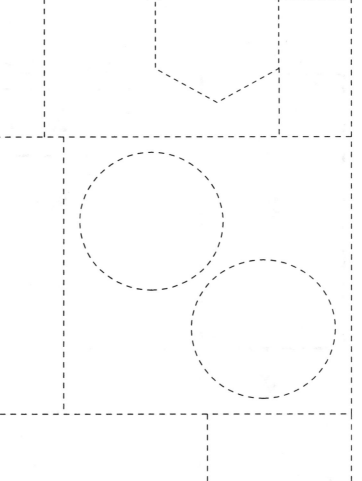

Block Bear

Name _____

➤ Cover the shapes with blocks, and show the teacher.

➤ Then color the design.

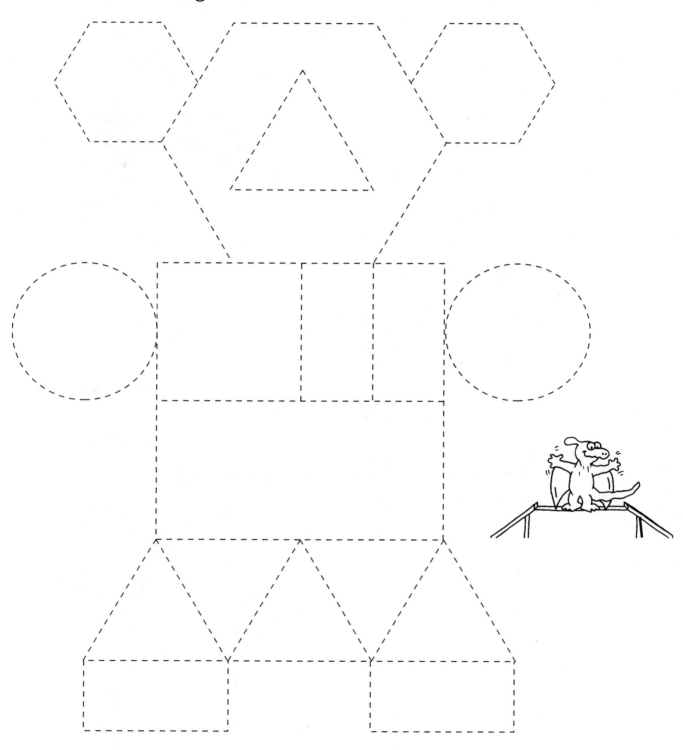

School

Name _____

➤ Make a school with blocks, and show the teacher.

➤ Color the school.

Fill the Square

➤ Fill the outlined square below with the number of blocks shown in the chart.

➤ Then record how many of each block you use.

Number of Blocks	■	▪	▮	▪
1				
2				
3				
4				
5				
6				
7				

Fill the Shape

Name_____

➤ Fill the outlined shape below with the number of blocks shown in the chart.

➤ Then record how many of each block you use.

Number of Blocks	⬢	⬡	▲	▴
3				
4				
6				
7				

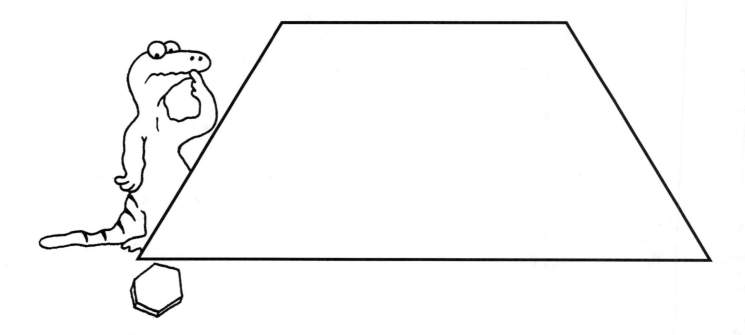

Fill It Up!

Name _____

➤ Fill the outlined shape below with the number of blocks shown in the chart.

➤ Then record how many of each block you used.

Number of Blocks	▲	▲	▮	▪	▪
3					
4					
5					
6					
6					
7					
8					
9					

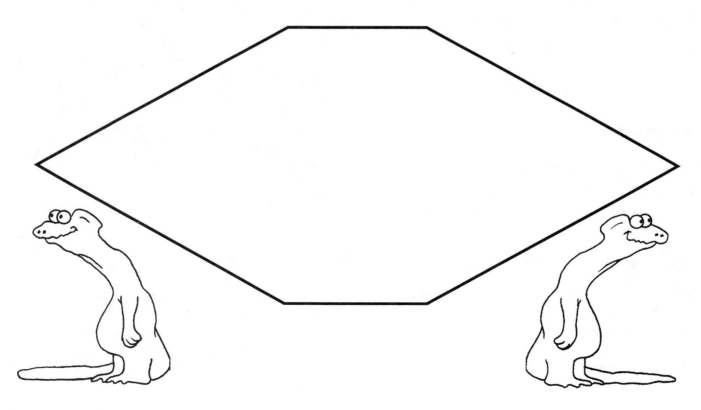

Relational Attribute Blocks
© 1993 Learning Resources, Inc.

Section C: More Shape Puzzles
Teaching Notes

Children learn to make larger sizes of square, rectangular, and triangular relational attribute blocks. They also examine other geometric shapes such as the *parallelogram*, *rhombus*, *pentagon*, and *trapezoid*. Other hexagonal shapes also are introduced.

With older children, discuss congruence and similarity of geometric shapes. *Congruent* figures have the same shape and size. *Similar* figures have the same shape, but are proportional in size.

Note: Children working in small groups may wish to combine two, three, or four sets of blocks to make large geometric shapes.

Objectives

- Make large relational attribute block shapes.
- Construct shapes similar or congruent to a given shape.
- Create other geometric shapes.

Vocabulary

Parallelogram, rhombus, pentagon, trapezoid, polygon, quadrilateral, congruent, similar

Warm-Up

Review block shapes. Ask students to match a block to an object of the same shape in the classroom. Before moving on, be sure children can describe each shape in terms of sides and angles.

Using the Activity Pages

Large Square (page 28)

Children need the large and small squares and rectangles to make squares *A* and *B* shown on pages 28 and 29. Ask children to make charts like those on pages 23-25 to record their solutions.

Larger Square (page 29)

Ask children if they can form a square larger than square *B*. Place small squares and large rectangles around square *B* (made of 4 large squares) and call it square *C*. The larger square will be 7½" by 7½". Challenge children to make an even larger square. Place the remaining small squares, large rectangles, and four small rectangles around square *C* to make a larger square. Call it square *D*, which measures 9" by 9". You may wish to have children use rulers to verify that the sides of each square are the same length.

Rectangles (page 30)

In this activity, children discover that for a larger rectangle to be similar to a rectangular block, its length must be twice as long as its width. On page 30, rectangles *G*, *J*, and *M* are similar to each other. When children make the same size shape using different blocks, they form *congruent* rectangles. Ask older children to make rectangles larger than *M* and specify if they are similar to it. *Note:* Rectangles measuring 3¾" by 7½", 4½" by 9", and 6" by 12" are larger, similar rectangles.

Large Triangles *(page 31)*

Children need the large and small blocks to form triangles *R, S, T,* and *U,* shown on page 31. Some children may use a large hexagon to form triangles *T* and *U. Note:* Challenge children to form a triangle larger than triangle *U.* Three large hexagons and seven small triangles will form a larger, similar equilateral triangle with 7½" sides.

Parallelograms *(page 32)*

Students need the large and small triangular blocks and the large hexagonal blocks to form the four parallelograms on page 32. Figures *Q* and *R* are special parallelograms. Each is called a *rhombus* because its sides are all equal. Figures *L* and *P* and figures *Q* and *R* are similar to each other. Ask children if they can make a larger parallelogram or rhombus.

Pentagons *(page 33)*

Pentagons are polygons with five sides. Rectangles, squares, triangles, and hexagons are needed to form figures *A* through *E* on page 33. Ask children to make pentagons larger than figures *D* and *E.* Ask which pentagons are similar to each other (*B* and *D, C* and *E*).

More Hexagons *(page 34)*

The hexagonal relational attribute block is *regular* because all of its sides are equal in length. Unlike the shape of the hexagonal block, the hexagons on page 34 are not regular. Before children begin the activities on page 34, challenge them to make a larger regular hexagon using three large hexagons and six small triangles.

After children finish the hexagons on this page, ask them to make larger hexagons using large and small squares, rectangles, and triangles. With older children, ask whether any of the larger hexagons are similar to figures *A, B, C,* or *D.*

Trapezoids *(page 35)*

Trapezoids are quadrilaterals with only one set of parallel sides. Have children construct the trapezoids shown on page 35, then record their solutions by drawing lines and coloring the figures. Ask them if they can make a larger trapezoid. Use three large hexagons and six small triangles.

Wrap-Up

Ask children to make a geometric shape that is larger than a block, a parallelogram, or a trapezoid. Challenge them to use the blocks and make a shape that is congruent or similar to a given shape.

Extension Activity

Ask children to form letters and numerals with the blocks. Encourage them to make as many letters from A to Z and as many digits from 0 to 9 as they can. Record and color each letter and numeral on a separate sheet of paper, then display them in the classroom.

Large Square

Name_____

➤ Make square *A* with the blocks.

A

Larger Square

Name_____

➤ Make square *B* with the blocks.

B

More for You

● Make a square larger than *B* and call it *C*.
● Make a square larger than *C* and call it *D*.

Rectangles

Name_____

➤ Make rectangles G, H, J, K, L, and M with the blocks.

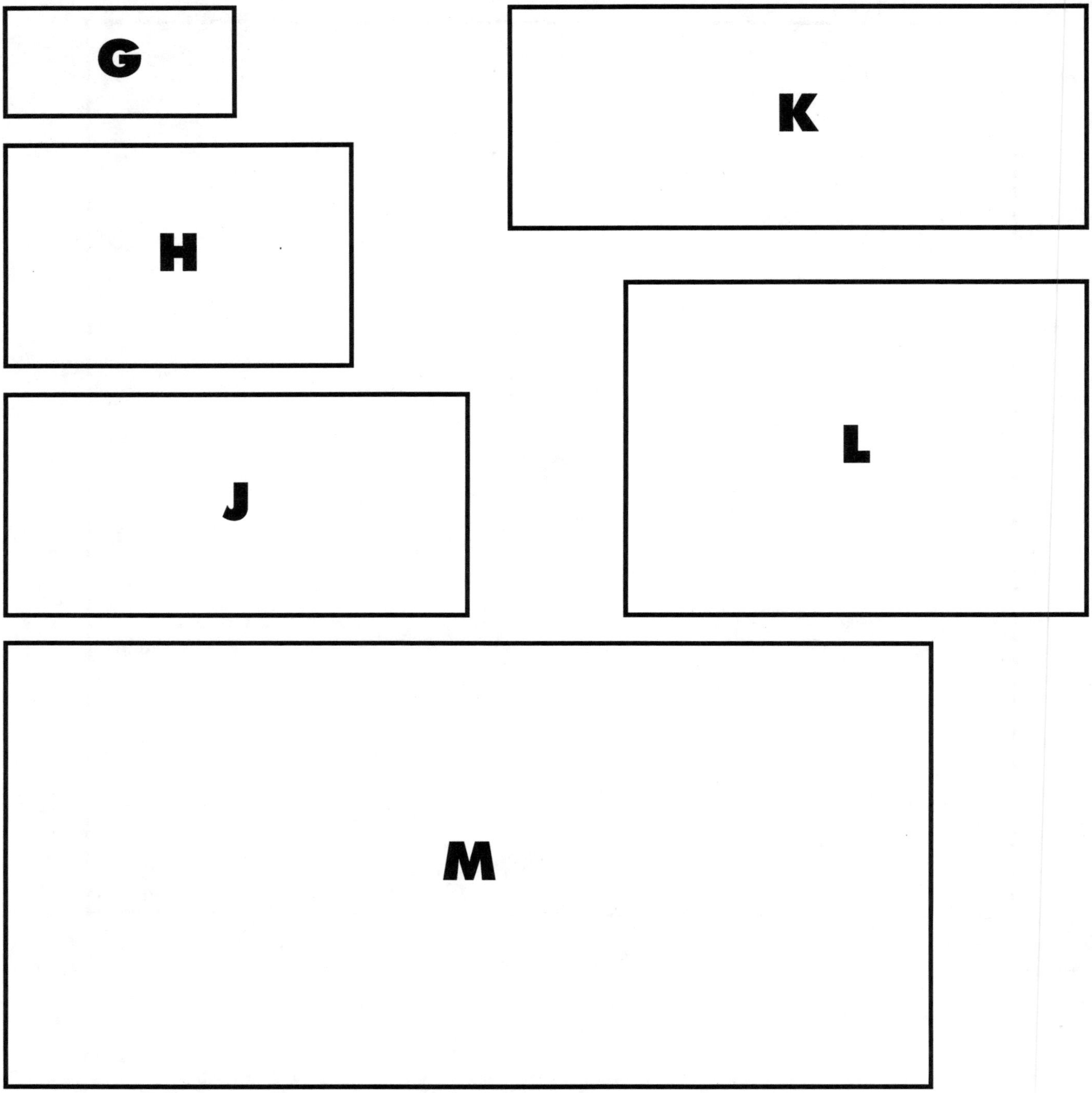

G

K

H

J

L

M

More for You

- Make a rectangle larger than M and label it N.
- Make a rectangle larger than N and label it P.

Large Triangles

➤ Make triangles *R, S, T,* and *U* with the blocks.

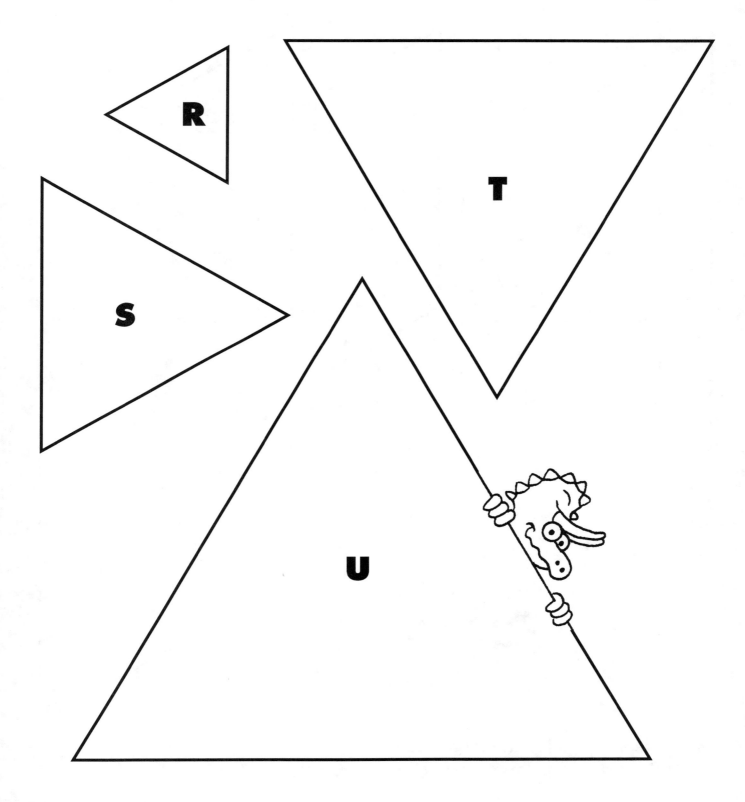

Parallelograms

Name _____

➤ Make parallelograms *P*, *Q*, *R*, and *L* with the blocks.

More for You

- Make a parallelogram larger than *L*.
- Make a rhombus larger than *R*.

Pentagons

Name _____

➤ Make pentagons *A*, *B*, *C*, *D*, and *E* with the blocks.

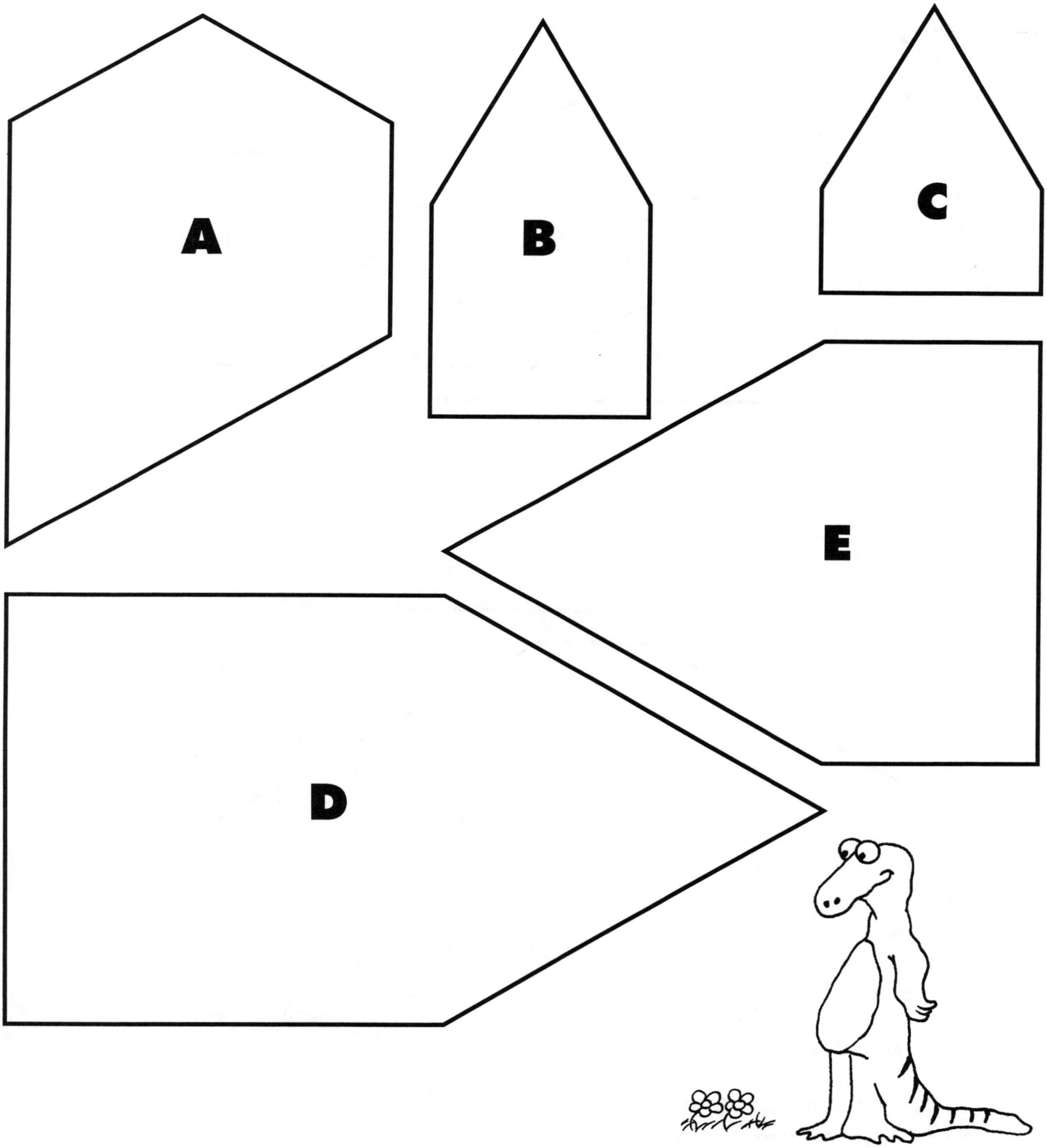

A

B

C

E

D

More Hexagons

➤ Make hexagons *A*, *B*, *C*, and *D* with the blocks.

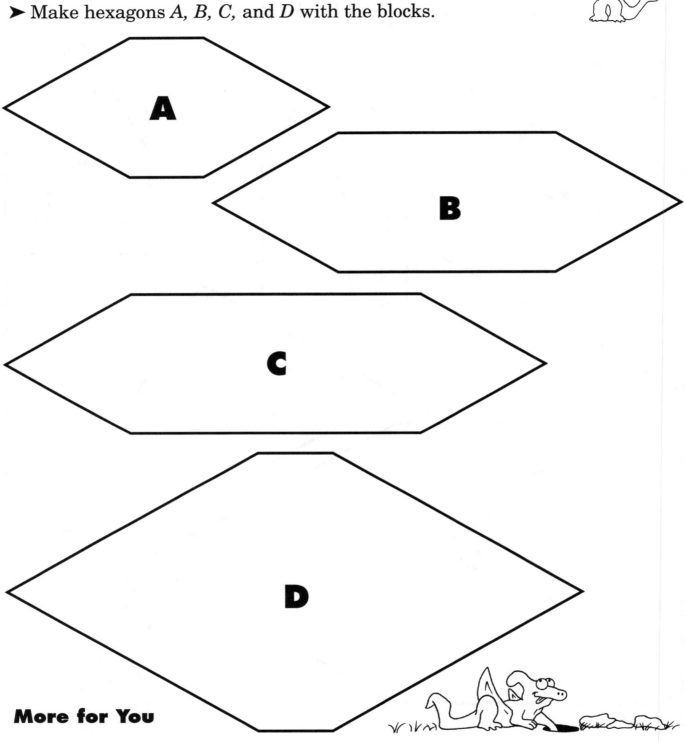

More for You

● Make a larger hexagon than those shown above.
● Make a large, regular hexagon.

Trapezoids

Name _____

➤ Make two trapezoids with the blocks.

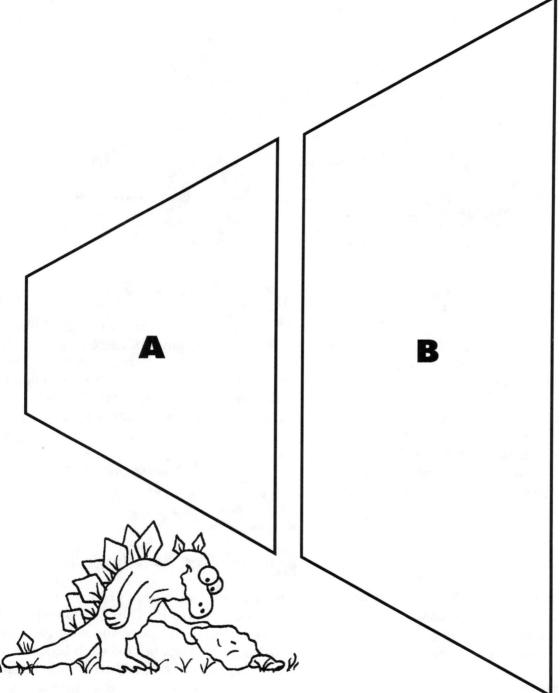

More for You

● Make a trapezoid larger than *B* and name it *C*.

Section D: Attribute Differences
Teaching Notes

In the following pages, students identify differences among the relational attribute blocks to solve problems. First, children compare a pair of blocks. Then they compare a sequence of blocks containing one, two, or three attribute differences.

Children need to see how two blocks are alike before they identify any differences. The word "zap" is used to mean *change* or *difference* from one block to another. A lightning graphic indicates a difference between the blocks.

Objectives

● Identify one, two, or three attribute differences between blocks.
● Sequence blocks with one, two, and/or three attribute differences.

Vocabulary

Alike, different, one-way zap, two-way zap, three-way zap

 ## Warm-Up

Show the class a pair of blocks. Ask how they are alike. Then ask how they are different. Show children one block and ask them to find a block that is different in only one way. There are many solutions for a "one-way zap."

 ## Using the Activity Pages

One-Way Zap *(page 39)*

Three blocks are displayed on page 39. For each block, help children find another block that is different in only one way. Several solutions are possible for each block. For example, for the small thin yellow circle, eight blocks have a one-attribute difference. One solution would be the *large* thin yellow circle.

⊙ One-Way Zap Map *(page 40)*

This activity requires children to find a one-way attribute difference for each succeeding block in the sequence. Note that the sequence goes in a clockwise direction, starting from the upper left corner. The fourth block also must have a one-way attribute difference in relationship to the first block.

Allow children to work in groups of two or three to complete the One-Way Zap Map. You or a child may decide the first block to be played. An example of a completed One-Way Zap Map is shown below.

▲ Two-Way Zap *(page 41)*

Page 41 is similar to page 39; however, this time children must find a block that is different in *two* ways from the block shown. There are 21 possible solutions for each block.

⬡ Two-Way Zap Map *(page 42)*

The Two-Way Zap Map is the same type of puzzle as the One-Way Zap Map, except that there must be a two-way difference between the blocks. See the completed example below.

One-Way Zap Map

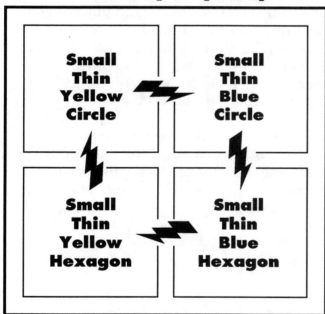

Two-Way Zap Map

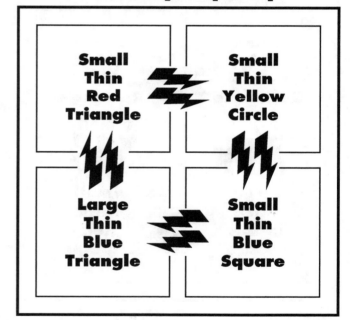

▲ Three-Way Zap (page 43)

Page 43 is similar to pages 39 and 41; however, this time children must find a block that is different in *three* ways from the block shown. There are 20 possible solutions for each block.

⬣ Three-Way Zap Map (page 44)

The Three-Way Zap Map is the same type of puzzle as the One-Way Zap Map, except that children must find a three-way difference between blocks. See example below.

Three-Way Zap Map

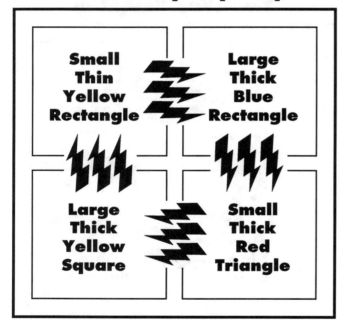

◎ One- and Two-Way Zap Map (page 45)

Children look for one- *and* two-way attribute differences between blocks.

▣ Zip-Zap Map (page 46)

Children look for one-, two-, *and* three-way attribute differences between blocks.

Wrap-Up

Students can work in groups of four to make one-way zap "trains." The first child selects a block and places it on the table. The second child chooses a block that is different in only one way and places it next to the first block. The third child then selects a block that is different in only one way from the second block.

Children choose blocks until they cannot find any other block with one difference, or until they run out of blocks. Repeat the activity using two- and three-way attribute differences.

Relational Attribute Blocks
© 1993 Learning Resources, Inc.

One-Way Zap

Name _____

➤ Find a block that is different in one way.

➤ Trace and color it. Draw a thick outline if it is a thick block.

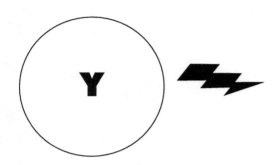

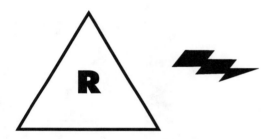

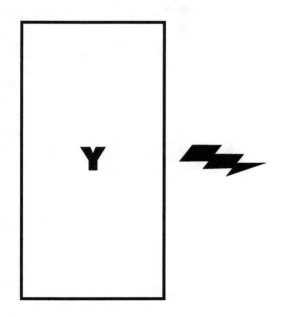

Use **THICK** and THIN blocks.

One-Way Zap Map

Name_____

➤ Choose a block and place it on "Start."

➤ Next, go from one space to another, and find blocks that have one-way differences.

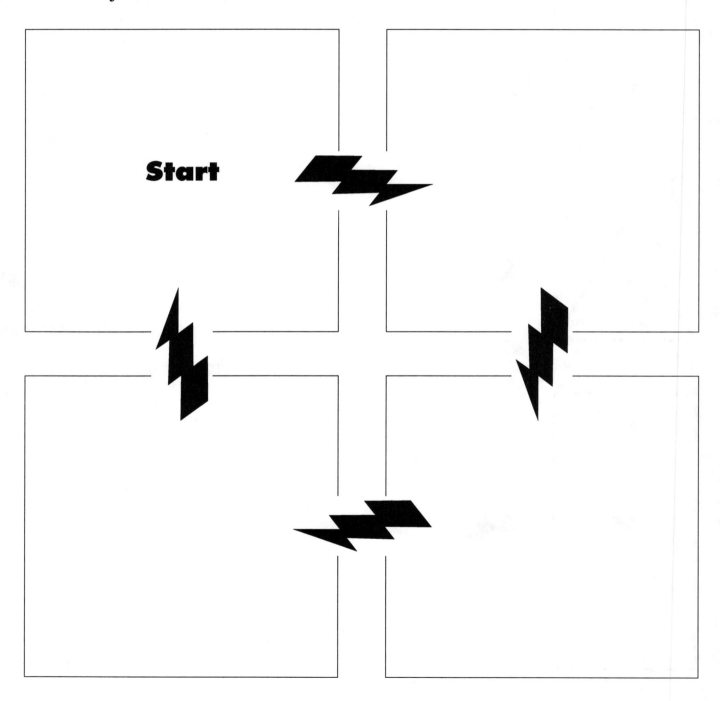

Start

Two-Way Zap

Name _____

➤ Find a block that is different in two ways.

➤ Trace and color it. Draw a thick outline if it is a thick block.

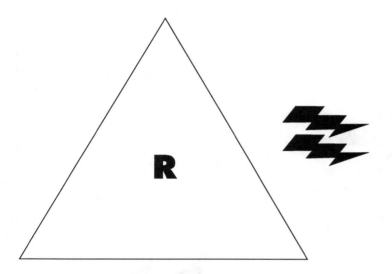

Use **THICK** and THIN blocks.

Two-Way Zap Map

Name_____

➤ Choose a block and place it on "Start."

➤ Next, go from one space to another, and find blocks that have two-way differences.

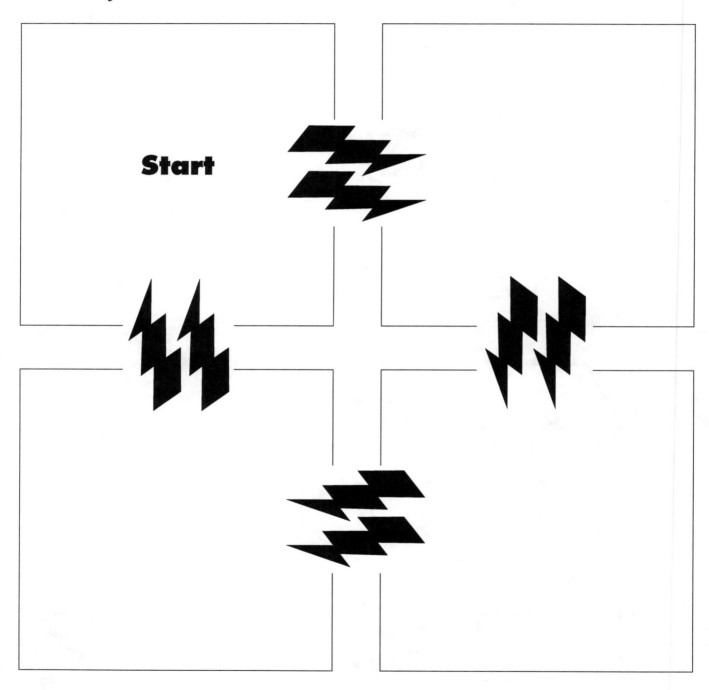

Start

Three-Way Zap

Name _____

➤ Find a block that is different in three ways.

➤ Trace and color it. Draw a thick outline if it is a thick block.

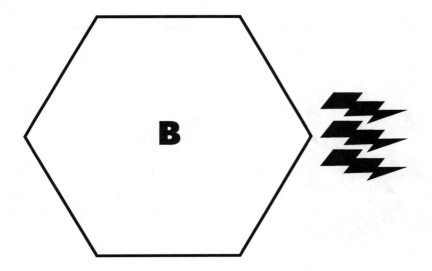

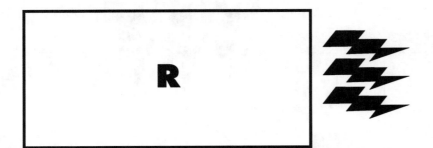

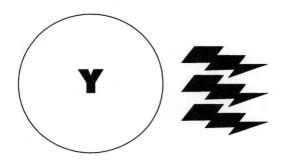

Use **THICK** and THIN blocks.

Three-Way Zap Map

Name _____

➤ Choose a block and place it on "Start."

➤ Next, go from one space to another, and find blocks that have three-way differences.

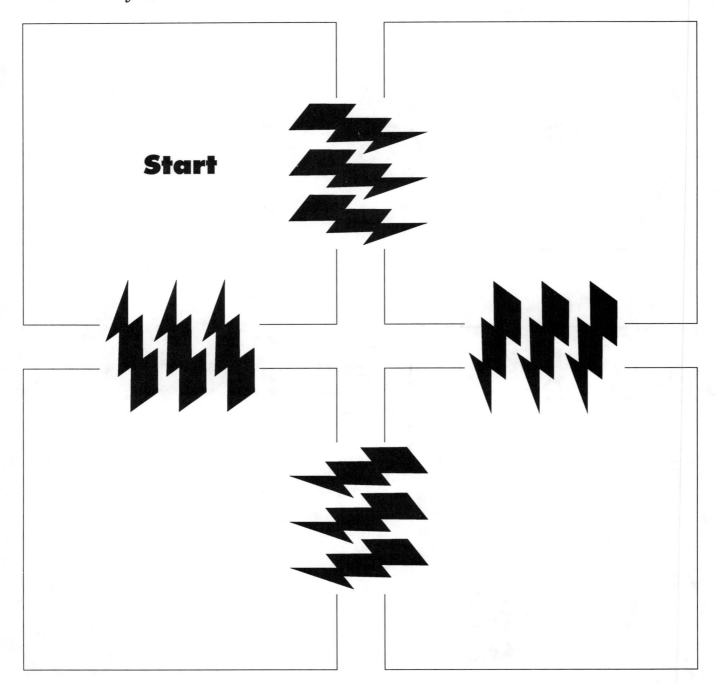

Start

One- and Two-Way Zap Map

Name _____

➤ Choose a block and place it on "Start."

➤ Next, go from one space to another, and find blocks that have two- and one-way differences.

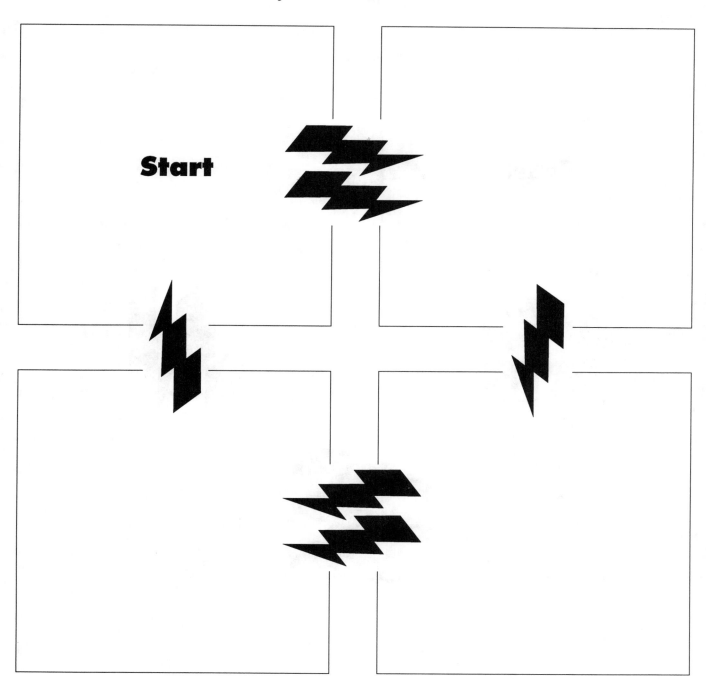

Start

Zip-Zap Map

Name _____

➤ Choose a block and place it on "Start."

➤ Next, go from one space to another, and find blocks
  that have one-, two-, and three-way differences.

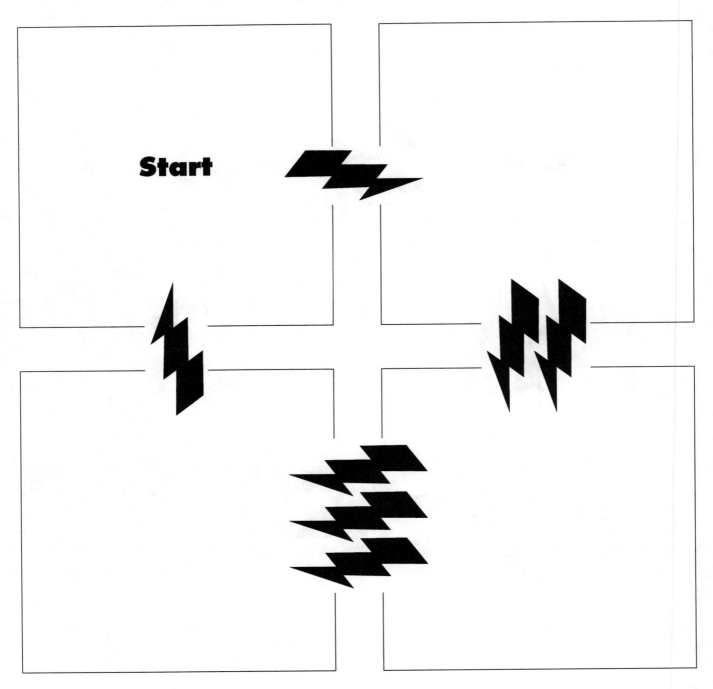

Relational Attribute Blocks
© 1993 Learning Resources, Inc.

Section E: Logic Problems
Teaching Notes

In this section on logic, children focus on attributes found in a set of blocks and those that are not. For example, a set of blocks that *is red* does not contain blocks that are blue or yellow.

By the same token, a set of blocks that *is not red* may include blue blocks, yellow blocks, or blue and yellow blocks. Children will be sorting several times to find the set or subset that satisfies the required attributes.

Mystery Block puzzles are both challenging and fun. These puzzles can be placed in a learning center or a math corner for children to use during free time. You can make the puzzles more durable by laminating them or pasting them on index cards.

Objectives

● To use visual perception and logical reasoning to solve problems.
● To sort blocks several times to solve problems.

Vocabulary

Mystery, puzzles, clues, is (are), is (are) not

 **Warm-Up**

These warm-up activities will help children get used to hearing "is" and "is not" connected with the blocks.

Direct children to perform sorting tasks such as the following:

● Find a set of blocks that is red (red blocks).
● Find a set of blocks that is not blue (red and yellow blocks).
● Find a set of blocks that is neither blue nor red (yellow blocks).
● Find a set of blocks that is round and not large (small circles).
● Find a set of blocks that is not thin, not small, and not red (large thick blue and yellow blocks).
● Find a set of blocks that is neither blue nor yellow (red blocks).
● Find a set of red blocks that have three sides on each block (red triangles).

 **Using the Activity Pages**

Students can work in pairs or in small groups to figure out solutions to the problems on the mystery cards. For Mystery Sets 1-12, and Mystery Block Puzzles A-M, have children cut out the cards, shuffle them, turn them face down, choose a card, and complete the task to solve the puzzle.

With some students, you may wish to work only with sets of four cards at a time at first, since each page of four cards focuses on a specific skill. As children work together, observe how they organize their thoughts as they listen to each other's explanations for solving the puzzles. All puzzles help improve children's vocabulary.

Mystery Sets 1-4 *(page 49)*

The cards in this set focus on the word *are*. Children are to find the set of blocks that satisfies the clues. After they have met the criteria, have them name the set using the attributes of size, shape, color, and thickness. You also may wish to have the children list or call out each block in the set.

Mystery Sets 5-8 *(page 50)*

The cards in this set focus on the words *are not*. Some children may have difficulty with this concept. Encourage them to talk to help them find attributes for the set. For example, if the set "is not round," it does not contain circles. It contains squares, rectangles, triangles, and hexagons (thick, thin, large, small, and in all three colors). Ask why some sets contain many blocks and why others contain only a few.

Mystery Sets 9-12 *(page 51)*

The clues on these cards combine the words *are* and *are not*.

Mystery Block Puzzles A-D *(page 52)*

These four cards reinforce the concept *is*. All clues direct the children to concentrate on specific block attributes.

Mystery Block Puzzles E-H *(page 53)*

These four cards reinforce the concept *is not*. All clues force the children to think of opposite or other attributes to determine the mystery block.

Mystery Block Puzzles J-M *(page 54)*

These four cards contain a combination of *is* and *is not* phrases. Children can create their own mystery block puzzles to challenge each other and gain experience in writing and problem solving.

Wrap-Up

Stack the cards for the Mystery Sets and Mystery Block Puzzles face down. Have a child select a card and find the appropriate set of blocks. Observe the child's problem-solving techniques.

Mystery Sets 1-4

Name _____

➤ Cut out the cards and find the mystery sets.

Mystery Set 1

The blocks are large.
The blocks are red.

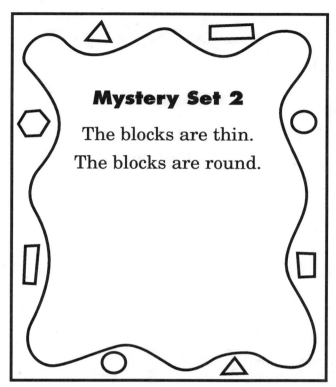

Mystery Set 2

The blocks are thin.
The blocks are round.

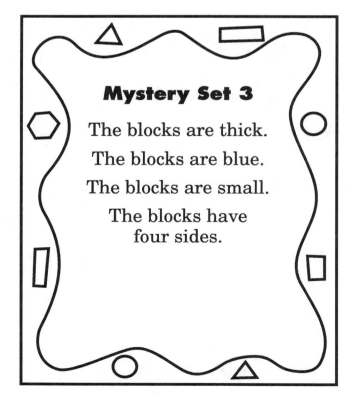

Mystery Set 3

The blocks are thick.
The blocks are blue.
The blocks are small.
The blocks have
four sides.

Mystery Set 4

The blocks are yellow.
The blocks are thin.
The blocks have more
than four sides.

Mystery Sets 5-8

Name _____

➤ Cut out the cards and find the mystery sets.

Mystery Set 5

The blocks do not have four sides.

Mystery Set 6

The blocks are not blue.

The blocks are not thin.

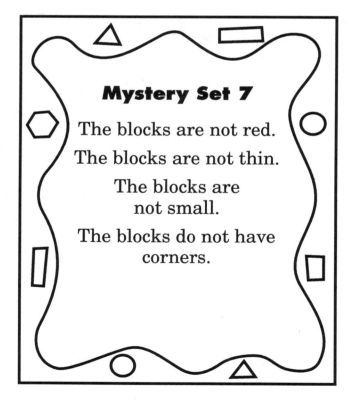

Mystery Set 7

The blocks are not red.

The blocks are not thin.

The blocks are not small.

The blocks do not have corners.

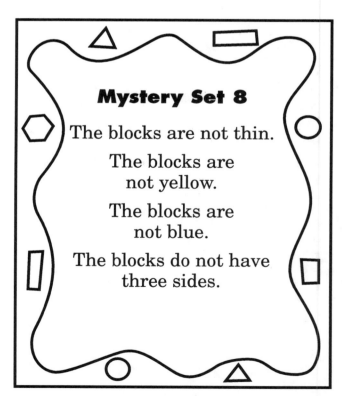

Mystery Set 8

The blocks are not thin.

The blocks are not yellow.

The blocks are not blue.

The blocks do not have three sides.

Mystery Sets 9-12

Name _____

➤ Cut out the cards and find the mystery sets.

Mystery Set 9

The blocks are large.

The blocks are
not regular.

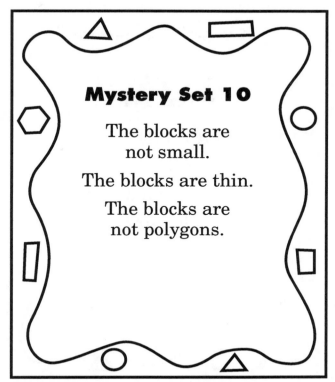

Mystery Set 10

The blocks are
not small.

The blocks are thin.

The blocks are
not polygons.

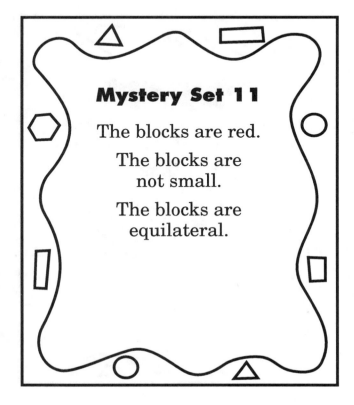

Mystery Set 11

The blocks are red.

The blocks are
not small.

The blocks are
equilateral.

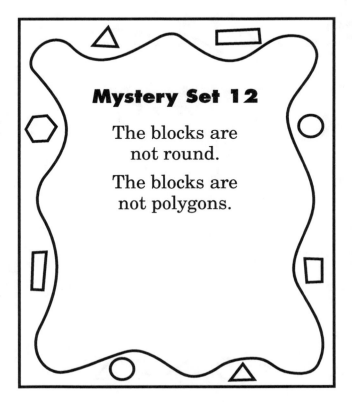

Mystery Set 12

The blocks are
not round.

The blocks are
not polygons.

Mystery Block Puzzles A-D

Name _____

➤ Cut out the cards and find the mystery blocks.

Mystery Block Puzzle A

It is blue.

It is large.

It is round.

It is thin.

Mystery Block Puzzle B

It is small.

It is yellow.

It is thick.

It has three sides.

Mystery Block Puzzle C

It is thick.

It is small.

It is red.

It has more than four sides.

Mystery Block Puzzle D

It is blue.

It is thin.

It is large.

It has four sides.

It is equilateral.

Name _____

➤ Cut out the cards and find the mystery blocks.

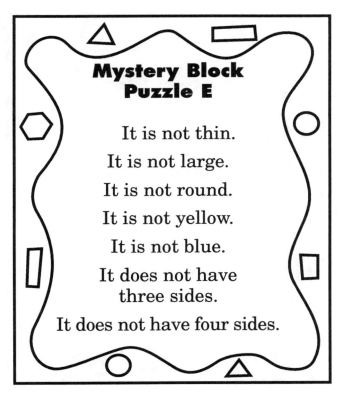

Mystery Block Puzzle E

It is not thin.

It is not large.

It is not round.

It is not yellow.

It is not blue.

It does not have three sides.

It does not have four sides.

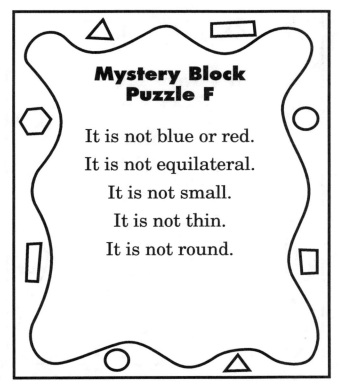

Mystery Block Puzzle F

It is not blue or red.

It is not equilateral.

It is not small.

It is not thin.

It is not round.

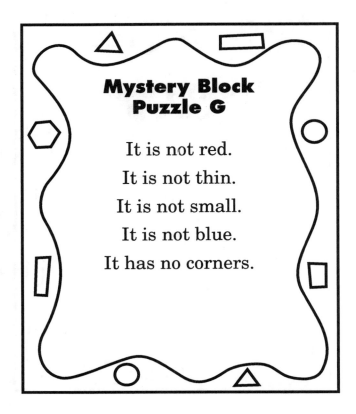

Mystery Block Puzzle G

It is not red.

It is not thin.

It is not small.

It is not blue.

It has no corners.

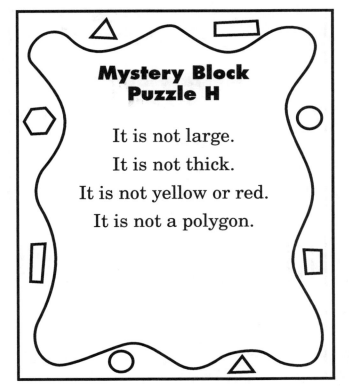

Mystery Block Puzzle H

It is not large.

It is not thick.

It is not yellow or red.

It is not a polygon.

Mystery Block Puzzles J-M

Name _____

➤ Cut out the cards and find the mystery blocks.

Mystery Block Puzzle J

It is thick.

It is blue.

It is not large.

It is round.

Mystery Block Puzzle K

It is not regular.

It is not small.

It is thin.

It is yellow.

It is not round.

Mystery Block Puzzle L

It is thin.

It is not blue.

It is small.

It is not red.

It has six sides.

Mystery Block Puzzle M

It is not thin.

It is not large.

It is blue.

It is regular.

It has pairs of equivalent opposite sides.

Section F: Making Arrangements
Teaching Notes

In this section, children deal with permutations of two or three blocks at a time. *A permutation of a set of blocks is each possible arrangement of the blocks.* Several figures are shown on each activity page. Caution students not to record a particular arrangement more than once.

This activity sharpens children's visual perception skills and demonstrates there are many solutions to a problem. As children complete the pages, cut out all the unique solutions and paste on 3" x 5" index cards. Place these activity cards and a set of blocks in a learning center so children may return during free time.

The following activity combines language arts and math. Give one pair of children three index cards and have them write one of the letters *A*, *T* and *C* on each of the cards. Direct them to arrange the cards to make a different letter sequence each time, and record each arrangement on a sheet of paper (ACT, ATC, CAT, CTA, TAC, TCA). Ask them how many arrangements of the letters they can make (6) and how many arrangements spell a word (2: ACT, CAT). Repeat this activity at another time, using other arrangements of three or more letters.

Objectives

● Arrange two blocks in various ways.
● Arrange three blocks in various ways.

Vocabulary

Arrangement, design

Warm-Up

Set three chairs in a row in the front of the room. Ask for three children (three girls, three boys, two boys and one girl, or one boy and two girls) to sit in the chairs. Record the seating arrangements by child's name on the chalkboard. Direct the children to seat and reseat themselves until they have found six different ways to be seated. If there is a combination of boys and girls, ask which seating arrangements allow two boys or two girls to sit next to each other.

Using the Activity Pages

Circle in a Square *(page 57)*

For this activity, use a circle and square of each color. Instruct children to find all six two-color arrangements for a small circle placed on a small square. When the children finish this activity, ask them in what other ways they can place the circle on the square. Ask what these arrangements would look like (one-color: red on red, blue on blue, yellow on yellow). Ask children whether they get the same results if they use large circles and large squares (yes).

◆Hexagon in a Circle (*page 58*)

Ask children to find all the two-color arrangements with a small hexagon on a small circle (6). Ask if there are any more arrangements (yes, three one-color arrangements). Ask children whether they get the same results if they use large circles with large hexagons. Ask about the size of the hexagon in relation to the size of the circle.

◆Hexagons, Circles, Squares (*page 59*)

This activity involves three shapes. Challenge children to find all possible arrangements of a small hexagon placed on a small circle placed on a small square. Ask how many arrangements have three colors (6), two colors (6), and one color (3).

●Circles in a Rectangle (*page 60*)

Using the six small circles and six large rectangles, have students find all the possible two- and three-color arrangements. Order is important. For example, there are two ways to make a three-color arrangement of yellow and blue circles on a red rectangle. Make two copies of page 60 for each child: one to record the two-color arrangements, and one to record the three-color arrangements.

●Circles, Hexagons, Rectangles (*page 61*)

This activity page is similar to page 60. Make two copies for each child: one to record the two-color arrangements and one to record the three-color arrangements.

●Circles in a Square (*page 62*)

Children will need three large squares, one of each color, and all six small circles for this activity. Make several copies of this page so children can record all possible arrangements.

▲Triangles in a Triangle (*page 63*)

Children need only small triangles to make these arrangements. There are two- and three-color "styles" (see *Solutions,* page 91).

▲Triangles in a Hexagon (*page 64*)

For this activity, children need all six small triangles and three large hexagons, one of each color. There are numerous solutions for this activity. Make several copies of this page so students can record all possible arrangements. Ask students whether some of the arrangements will be the same if the hexagon is rotated.

▲Triangle-Hexagon-Circle-Square (*page 65*)

The Triangle-Hexagon-Circle-Square challenges children to find all possible puzzle arrangements of the blocks using large squares, large circles, and large hexagons with small triangles. Make several copies of this page so children can record all possible answers.

After completing the activity page, have students cut out their solutions and make a set of activity cards to exchange with each other. You may wish to make this activity a class project, then bind solutions into a book.

Wrap-Up

Children can use three different hats, vests, and masks to show all possible permutations of dress. Students may wish to name the "characters" for each arrangement, draw the characters, take pictures with a camera, or even make a videotape of the possibilities.

Circle in a Square

Name_____

➤ Show the different ways to arrange a small circle
  on a small square.

➤ Color the figures below to record your answers.

Hexagon in a Circle

Name _____

➤ Show the different ways to arrange a small hexagon on a small circle.

➤ Color the figures below to record your answers.

Relational Attribute Blocks
© 1993 Learning Resources, Inc.

Hexagons, Circles, Squares

Name_____

➤ Show the different ways to arrange a small hexagon
on a small circle on a small square.

➤ Color the figures below to record your answers.

Circles in a Rectangle

Name_____

➤ Show the different ways to arrange two small circles
  on a large rectangle.

➤ Color the figures below to record your answers.

Circles, Hexagons, Rectangles

Name _____

➤ Show the different ways to arrange a small circle and
a small hexagon on a large rectangle.

➤ Color the figures to record your answers.

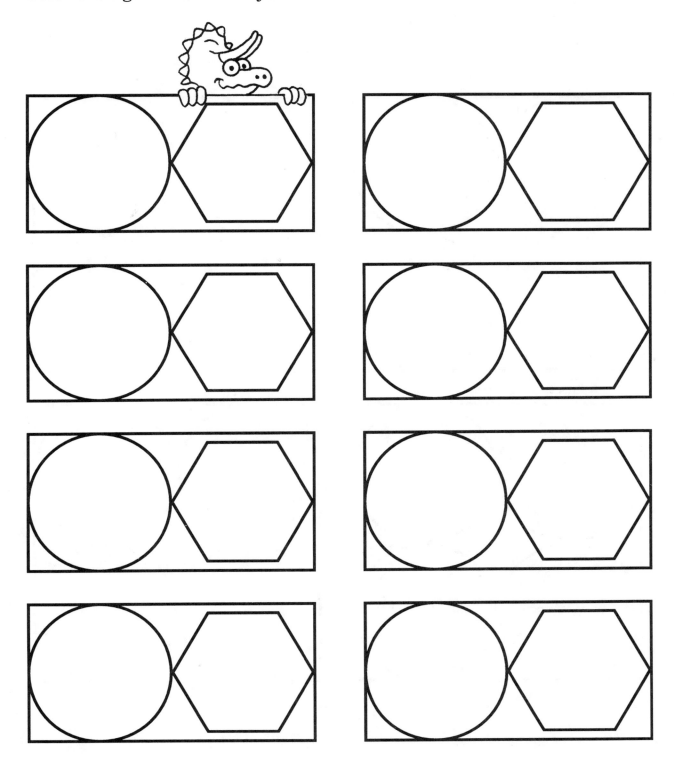

Circles in a Square

Name _____

➤ Show the different ways to arrange four small circles on a large square.

➤ Color the figures below to record your answers.

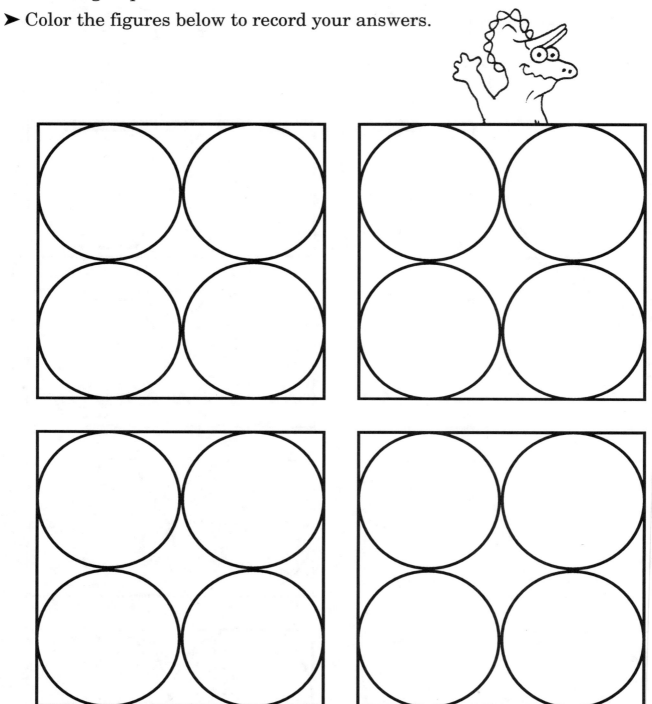

Relational Attribute Blocks
© 1993 Learning Resources, Inc.

Triangles in a Triangle

Name _____

➤ Show the different ways to arrange four small triangles on a large triangle.

➤ Color the figures below to record your answers.

Relational Attribute Blocks
© 1993 Learning Resources, Inc.

Triangles in a Hexagon

Name _____

➤ Show the different ways to arrange six small triangles
  on a large hexagon.

➤ Color the figures below to record your answers.

Triangle-Hexagon-Circle-Square

Name _____

➤ Show the different ways to arrange six small triangles on a large hexagon on a large circle on a large square.

➤ Color the figures below to record your answers.

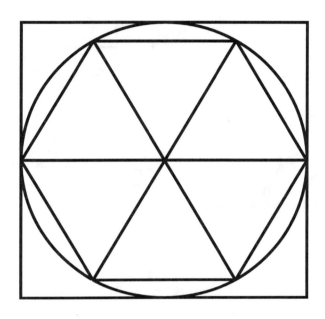
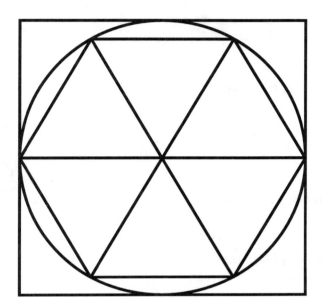
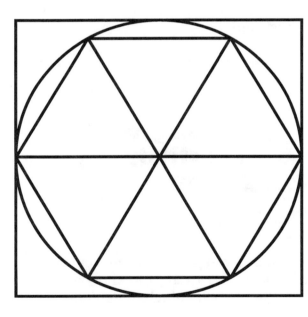
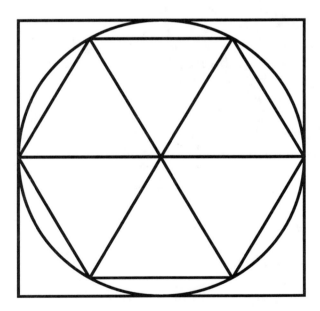

Section G: Shapes and Fractions
Teaching Notes

In this section, students identify fractional parts of the blocks and then name fractional parts formed by several blocks. When students learn to combine fractional parts into a whole region, they actually learn to add fractions.

Objectives

- Identify a fractional part of an object.
- Show a fractional part of an object.

Vocabulary

Fraction, one half, one third, thirds, one fourth, fourths, one sixth, sixths, one eighth, eighths

Warm-Up

Here is a fold-and-color activity to help children learn about fractional parts. Distribute three 3" x 3" squares of paper to each child. Instruct them to fold the square in half, color half of it, and then label it ½. Fold the other two squares of paper to show the fractions ¼ and ⅛. After children understand how the fractional parts look on the squares of paper, have them compare the colored portions of their squares with the relational attribute blocks.

Students should make the following discoveries:
- The large rectangle is ½ of the large square.
- The small square is ¼ of the large square.
- The small rectangle is ⅛ of the large square.

Discuss other relationships such as:

- The small square is ½ of the large rectangle.
- The small rectangle is ¼ of the large rectangle.

Challenge older children to show ¾ or ⅝ of a region using the blocks.

Using the Activity Pages

Halves *(page 68)*

This activity explores the concept of *one half.* Demonstrate how to show a fractional part of a block by placing a smaller block on a larger block. Compare and discuss problems 1 and 4. You can cover half of a block using more than one smaller block.

Fourths (page 69)

Discuss the concept of *one fourth* using the blocks. Show how a small square is ¼ of a large square and a small rectangle is ¼ of a large rectangle. Extend the discussion to include ²⁄₄ and ¾ of a region using small squares with a large square, small rectangles with a large rectangle, or small triangles with a large triangle. The problems on page 69 require children to show ¼, ²⁄₄, and ¾ of blocks. Using the small size shapes, challenge children to find ⅛, ⅜, ⅝, and ⅞ of the large squares and rectangles.

Thirds and Sixths (page 70)

Discuss the concepts of *one third* and *one sixth* using a large hexagon and the small triangles. Show ⅙, ²⁄₆, ³⁄₆, and so on. Ask children how they would show ½ (use 3 small triangles). Ask children how they would show ⅓ (use 2 small triangles) and ⅔ (use 4 small triangles). Make sure children understand how to use the blocks to show thirds and sixths before assigning page 70.

Cover Up (page 71)

On page 71, a specific number of blocks is used to cover each figure with a fractional amount of color. Children record their answers by tracing around the blocks and then coloring the appropriate parts of the figure. With older children, show how the figures on this page can be used to show addition: ½ + ½ = 1 and ½ + ¼ + ¼ = 1.

Cover Parts (page 72)

On this page, a specific number of blocks is used to cover figures showing halves, fourths, thirds, and sixths. Children record their answers by tracing around the blocks and then coloring the appropriate parts of the figure. Ask older children to write addition problems such as ½ + ⅓ + ⅙ = 1.

Cover Again (page 73)

This page is similar to pages 71 and 72, but children can determine the number of blocks to be used. With older students write an addition equation such as ¾ + ⅛ + ⅛ = 1 on the chalkboard or overhead projector. Ask them to use their blocks to create a figure for the equation. *Note:* A possible solution would be a large blue rectangle and a small blue square to make ¾ blue, and a small yellow rectangle and a small red rectangle to show ⅛ and ⅛.

Show Fractional Parts (page 74)

This activity requires children to make a shape showing fractional parts of color using a specific number of blocks. There may be more than one solution to each problem. For older children, relate these exercises to adding fractions using equations. *Note:* Provide 4 copies of this page, one for each problem.

More Fractional Parts (page 75)

This activity is similar to page 74, except the number of blocks to be used is not stated. Encourage children to find more than one solution for each problem. Have older children write a fraction addition equation next to each figure. *Note:* Provide 4 copies of this page, one for each problem.

Wrap-Up

Make a block figure using two or three colors. Ask students which fraction of the figure is a certain color. Or a child can make a figure of his or her own and then tell you how much of it is blue, yellow, or red.

Halves

Name _____

➤ Trace around the blocks, and then color them to show your answers.

➤ Write a fraction in the blank.

1. Cover the large square with a large rectangle.
   How much is covered? _____

2. Cover the large rectangle with a small square.
   How much is covered? _____

3. Cover the small square with a small rectangle.
   How much is covered? _____

4. Cover the large square with two small squares.
   How much is covered? _____

Fourths

Name _____

➤ Trace around the blocks, and then color them to show your answers.

➤ Write a fraction in the blank.

1. Cover the large square with
   a small square.
   How much is covered? _____

2. Cover the large triangle with
   three small triangles.
   How much is covered? _____

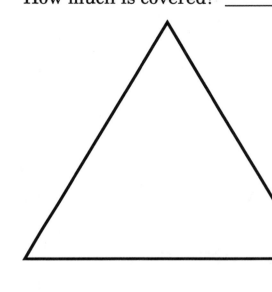

3. Cover the large rectangle with
   a small rectangle.
   How much is covered? _____

4. Cover the large square with
   two small rectangles.
   How much is covered? _____

Thirds and Sixths

Name _____

➤ Trace around the blocks, and then color them to show your answers.

➤ Write a fraction in the blank.

1. Cover the large hexagon with one small triangle.
   How much is covered? _____

2. Cover the large hexagon with five small triangles.
   How much is covered? _____

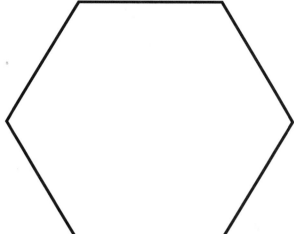

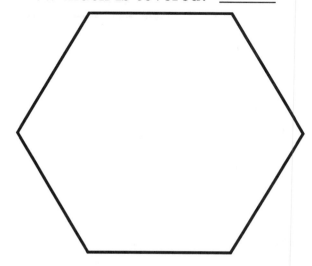

3. Cover the large hexagon with three small triangles.
   How much is covered? _____

4. Cover the large hexagon with two small triangles.
   How much is covered? _____

Relational Attribute Blocks
© 1993 Learning Resources, Inc.

Cover Up

Name _____

➤ Trace around the blocks, and then color them to show your answers.

1. Use two blocks to show
   $\frac{1}{2}$ blue and $\frac{1}{2}$ red.

2. Use three blocks to show
   $\frac{1}{2}$ blue, $\frac{1}{4}$ red, $\frac{1}{4}$ yellow.

3. Use four blocks to show
   $\frac{1}{2}$ yellow and $\frac{1}{2}$ red.

4. Use four blocks to show
   $\frac{1}{2}$ red, $\frac{1}{4}$ blue, $\frac{1}{4}$ yellow.

Cover Parts

Name _____

➤ Trace around the blocks, and then color them to show your answers.

1. Use three blocks to show $\frac{3}{4}$ blue and $\frac{1}{4}$ red.

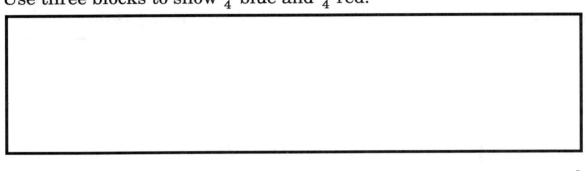

2. Use four blocks to show $\frac{1}{2}$ red, $\frac{1}{3}$ blue, and $\frac{1}{6}$ yellow.

3. Use six blocks to show $\frac{1}{3}$ red, $\frac{1}{3}$ yellow, and $\frac{1}{3}$ blue.

Cover Again

Name _____

➤ Use as many blocks as you wish to cover each figure.

➤ Trace around the blocks, and then color them to show your answers.

1. Show $\frac{1}{4}$ blue, $\frac{1}{2}$ red, $\frac{1}{4}$ yellow.

2. Show $\frac{1}{3}$ blue, $\frac{1}{3}$ yellow, and $\frac{1}{3}$ red.

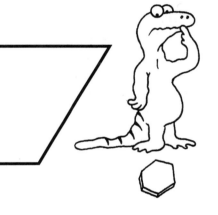

3. Show $\frac{3}{4}$ blue and $\frac{1}{4}$ red.

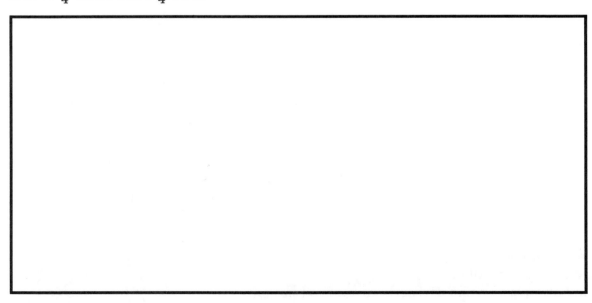

Show Fractional Parts

Name _____

➤ Trace around the blocks you choose, and then color them to show your answers.

1. Use four blocks to show $\frac{1}{4}$ red, $\frac{1}{4}$ blue, and $\frac{1}{2}$ yellow.

2. Use three blocks to show $\frac{1}{4}$ red, $\frac{1}{4}$ yellow, and $\frac{1}{2}$ blue.

3. Use six blocks to show $\frac{1}{4}$ red, $\frac{1}{2}$ yellow, and $\frac{1}{4}$ blue.

4. Use five blocks to show $\frac{3}{4}$ blue and $\frac{1}{4}$ yellow.

Hint: Use 4 copies of this page.
Label each page a number 1-4.
Show your answers on the correctly numbered page.

More Fractional Parts

Name _____

➤ Construct each figure using as many shapes as you wish from one set of blocks. Trace around the blocks, and then color them to show your answers.

1. Make a figure that is $\frac{2}{3}$ blue and $\frac{1}{3}$ red.

2. Make a figure that is $\frac{1}{3}$ yellow, $\frac{1}{3}$ red, and $\frac{1}{3}$ blue.

3. Make a figure that is $\frac{3}{4}$ blue, $\frac{1}{8}$ red, and $\frac{1}{8}$ yellow.

4. Make a figure that is $\frac{5}{6}$ blue and $\frac{1}{6}$ yellow.

Hint: Use 4 copies of this page.
Label each page a number 1-4.
Show your answers on the correctly numbered page.

Section H: Perimeter and Area
Teaching Notes

In this section, students use counting and measurement to find the perimeter and area of each relational attribute block. They also compare the perimeter or area of two blocks of the same shape when one of the block's dimensions is doubled. Older children can measure some of the blocks

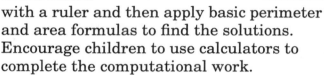

with a ruler and then apply basic perimeter and area formulas to find the solutions. Encourage children to use calculators to complete the computational work.

Objectives

● Find the perimeter of each block.
● Find the area of each block.

Vocabulary

Measurement, units, inches, centimeters, ruler, length, perimeter, circumference, area, side, height, diameter, radius, pi (π)

Perimeter

Perimeter is the distance around a figure. Its measure is given in terms of a standard unit such as an inch, a foot, or a centimeter, or a nonstandard unit such as the length of a paper clip or the side of a block. Rulers and tape measures are used to find perimeter. Measurements and the application of perimeter formulas are often combined to determine the perimeter of a figure. Students can use string to help find the perimeter of more complex figures, especially curved ones. *The distance around a circle is the circumference.*

Warm-Up

Find perimeter using nonstandard units. Distribute small paper clips and the large blocks to children. Show them how to place the paper clips around each shape. Then have students count the total number. For the large circle, have children place their paper clips around the outside of the circle and then around the inside, as shown:

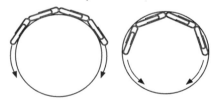

Explain that more paper clips are needed for the outside measurement than for the inside one. Children also should realize that the actual circumference of the circle is between the two paper clip lengths.

Using the Activity Pages

Counting Around *(page 79)*

Outlines of the large blocks are shown on page 79. Have children use the side of the small square as a unit of measure to find the perimeter of each block. Have children mark off each unit around the blocks as shown at right. The perimeter will be given as "units." Remind children that the perimeter of a circle is called the *circumference*. Students may have to give an estimate to the nearest whole unit for each figure.

Counting Around Again *(page 80)*

Outlines of selected large and small blocks are shown on page 80. Have children use the side of the small hexagon as a nonstandard unit of measure to find the perimeter of each block. Use the same measuring technique as on page 79. Ask children to compare the perimeters of the large blocks on pages 79 and 80. Ask why the measurements of the perimeters of the large blocks are twice as large on page 80 as on page 79. (The unit of measure for page 80 is half the size of the unit of measure for page 79.) Ask children if it was easier to find the circumference of the circle with the smaller units of measure.

Perimeter in Inches *(page 81)*

Ask children to find the perimeter of each block by measuring each side with an inch ruler. They can record their measurements on page 81. Ask children how they can use string and a ruler to find the perimeter of each block, especially the circumference of the circle. Older children can apply measurements to perimeter formulas to find the distance around each block. Then they can compare their calculations to the actual measurements.

Perimeter in Centimeters *(page 82)*

Direct children to find the perimeter of each block by measuring each side with a centimeter ruler. Have them record their measurements on page 82. Ask older children to compare calculated perimeters with the perimeters found by measuring around each block with a ruler. Children may measure each block to the nearest centimeter or tenth of a centimeter.

Area

Area is the amount of surface on an object or within a plane figure. Area is measured in square units such as square inches (sq. in.) or square centimeters (cm^2). Beginning work with area usually involves covering a plane figure with same-size shapes such as the small square blocks. If the small square is used as a nonstandard unit of measure, then covering the large square with four small squares yields a measurement of "four small squares." If one-inch squares were used to cover the large square, nine one-inch squares would be needed, and so the measurement would be "nine square inches."

Warm Up

Find area using nonstandard units. Using one-centimeter units from a set of base ten blocks, give ten to each child along with the large blocks. Direct children, either in pairs or small groups, to cover each large block with the centimeter squares. Encourage children to give the best estimate for the area of each block. Have them record and compare their findings with other children.

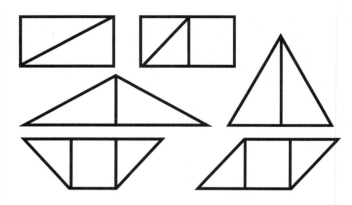

Estimating area. Here is a way to estimate the area of a large block when some of the small squares extend outside the block.

1. Count how many small squares extend outside the large block. *Suppose 24 squares fall partly outside the large block.*

2. Find half that number. *Half of 24 is 12.*

3. Count how many small squares are completely inside the large block. *Suppose 18 small squares are completely inside.*

4. Add the two numbers. *12 +18 = 40. An estimate for the area is 40.*

Using the Activity Pages

Area Cover-Up *(page 83)*

Direct children to use the small square as the unit of measure to find the area of each figure on page 83. Do any of the figures have the same area? Ask children how they figured out the area of the last figure.

Another Area Cover-Up *(page 84)*

Have children use the small triangle as the unit of measure to find the area of each figure. Ask if any of the figures have the same area. To help children understand that two figures can have the same areas but different shapes, have them cut out three copies of each of the following rectangles:

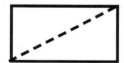 

By rearranging the pieces, they can see that figures can have the same area but different shapes as shown:

Area in Inches *(page 85)*

On page 85, the shaded regions shown on inch grid paper represent the large and small blocks. Use the method in the warm-up to estimate each area in square inches. Encourage older children to calculate area using the formulas, then compare the numbers to their estimated answers. Ask children to compare the area of a large block with its smaller counterpart such as a large square with a small square. Point out that when the dimensions of a figure are doubled, the area is four times as large.

Area in Centimeters *(page 86)*

On page 86, the shaded regions shown on centimeter grid paper represent the large and small blocks. Have children use the method in the warm-up to estimate each area in square centimeters. Older children can use measurements and area formulas to calculate the area of each block. Then ask them to compare these calculations with their estimates.

Wrap-Up

Students work in pairs using centimeter or inch graph paper. Ask one partner to draw a closed figure. Challenge the other student to find the perimeter and area of the figure. Then they can work together to agree on a solution.

Counting Around

Name _____

➤ Find the perimeter of each block using the side
of the small square as a unit of measure.

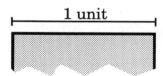

P = _____ units

P = _____ units

P = _____ units

C = _____ units

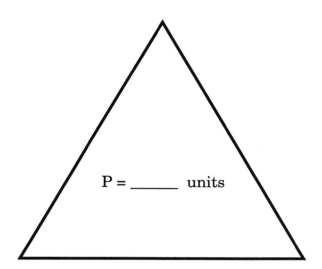

P = _____ units

Counting Around Again

Name _____

➤ Find the perimeter of each block using the side
of the small hexagon as a unit of measure.

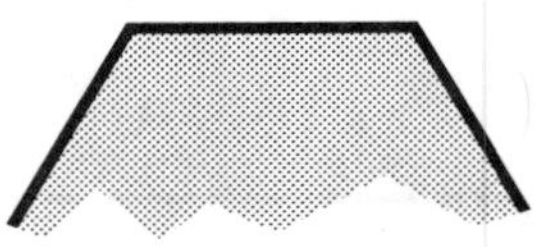

1 unit

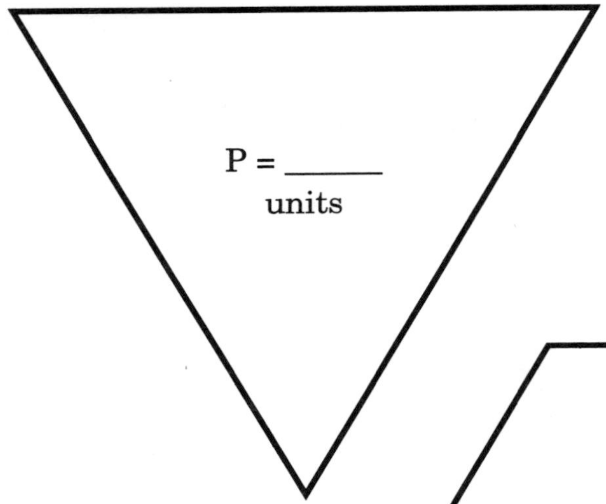

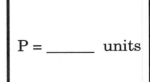

P = _____
units

P = _____ units

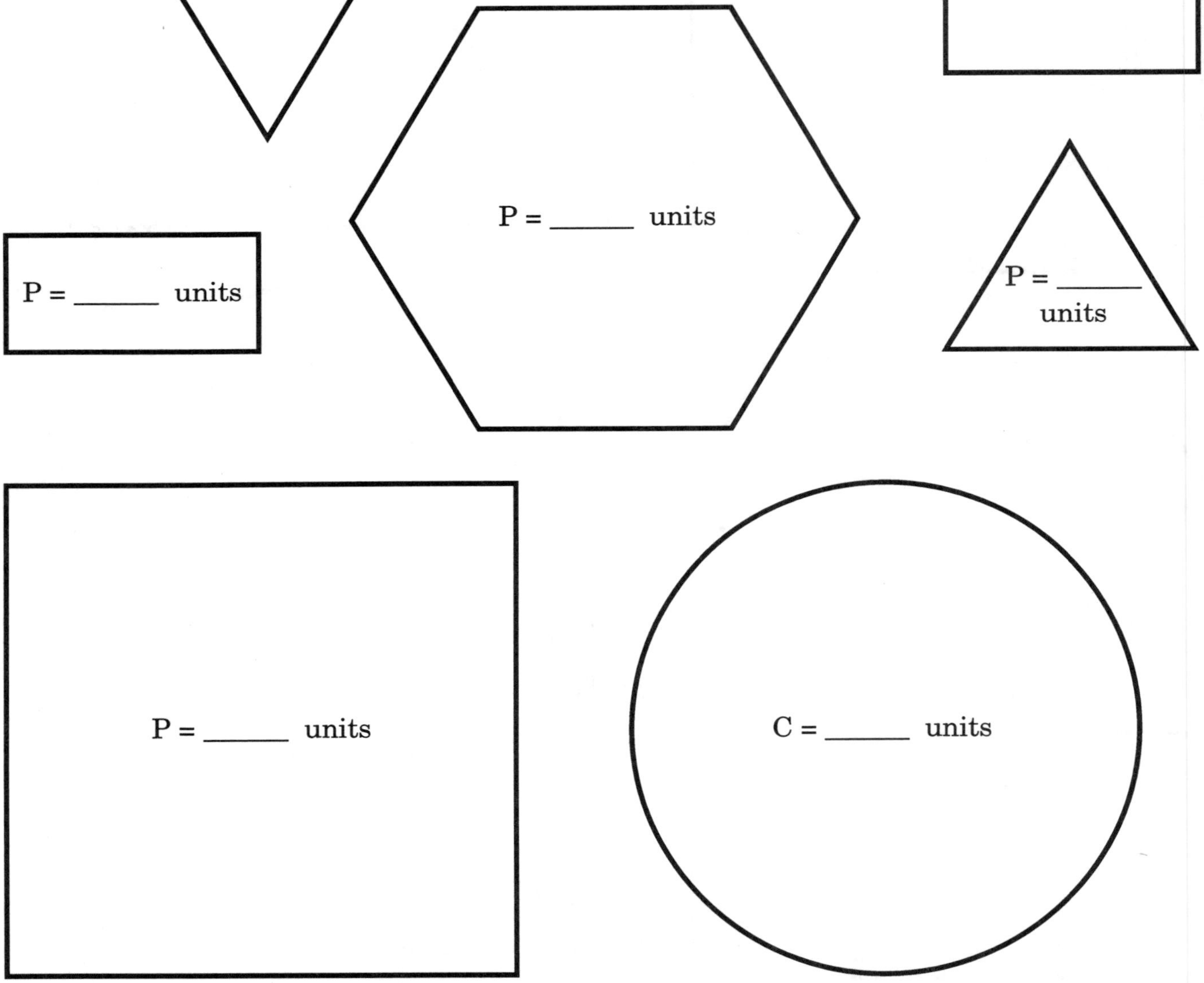

P = _____ units

P = _____ units

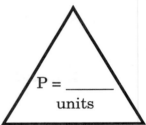

P = _____ units

P = _____
units

P = _____ units

C = _____ units

Perimeter in Inches

Name _____

➤ Find the perimeter of each block using a ruler marked in inches.
➤ Write the perimeter inside each block.

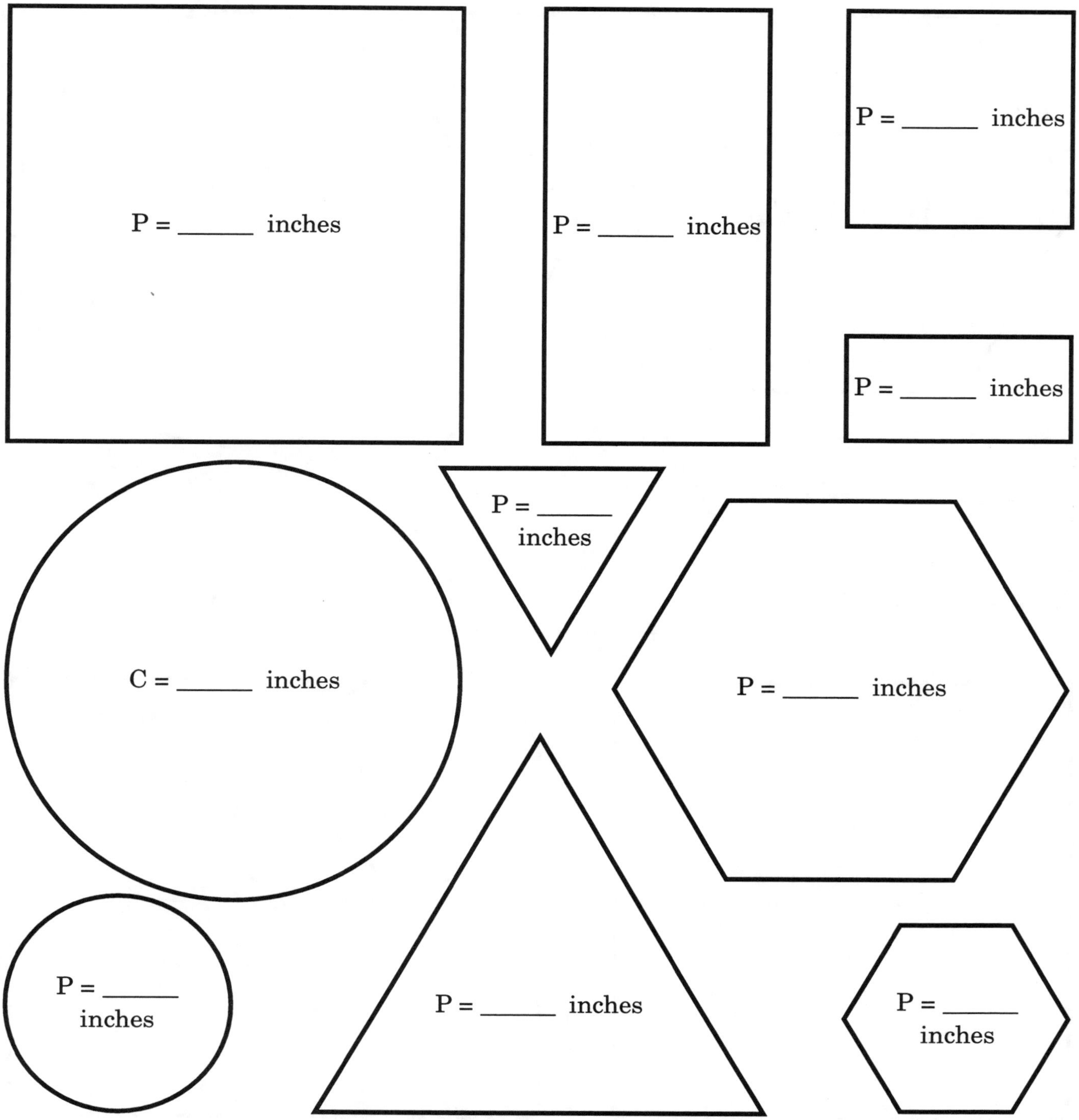

P = _____ inches

P = _____ inches

P = _____ inches

P = _____ inches

C = _____ inches

P = _____
_____ inches

P = _____ inches

P = _____
inches

P = _____ inches

P = _____
inches

Perimeter in Centimeters

Name _____

➤ Find the perimeter of each block using a ruler marked in centimeters.

➤ Write the perimeter inside each block.

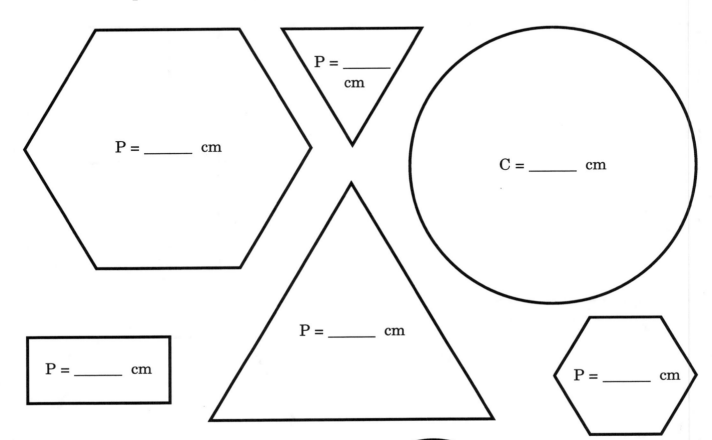

P = _____ cm

P = _____ cm

C = _____ cm

P = _____ cm

P = _____ cm

P = _____ cm

P = _____ cm

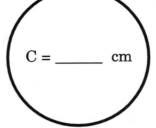

C = _____ cm

P = _____ cm

P = _____ cm

P = _____ cm

Area Cover-Up

Name _____

➤ Use small squares to find the area of each figure.

A

A = _____ small squares

B

A = _____ small squares

C

A = _____ small squares

D

A = _____ small squares

Another Area Cover-Up

Name _____

➤ Use small triangles to find the area of each figure.

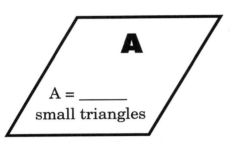

A = _____ small triangles

A = _____ small triangles

A = _____ small triangles

A = _____ small triangles

A = _____ small triangles

Area in Inches

Name _____

➤ For each shape, count the squares and parts of squares to find
the area of each block.

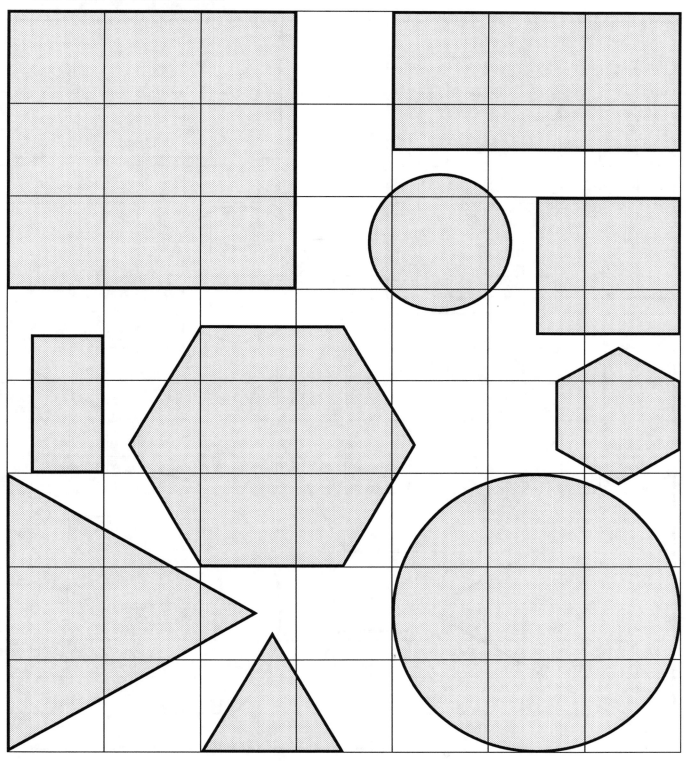

Area in Centimeters

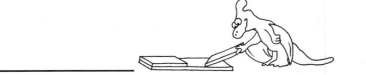

Name _____

➤ For each shape, count the squares and parts of squares to find the area of each block.

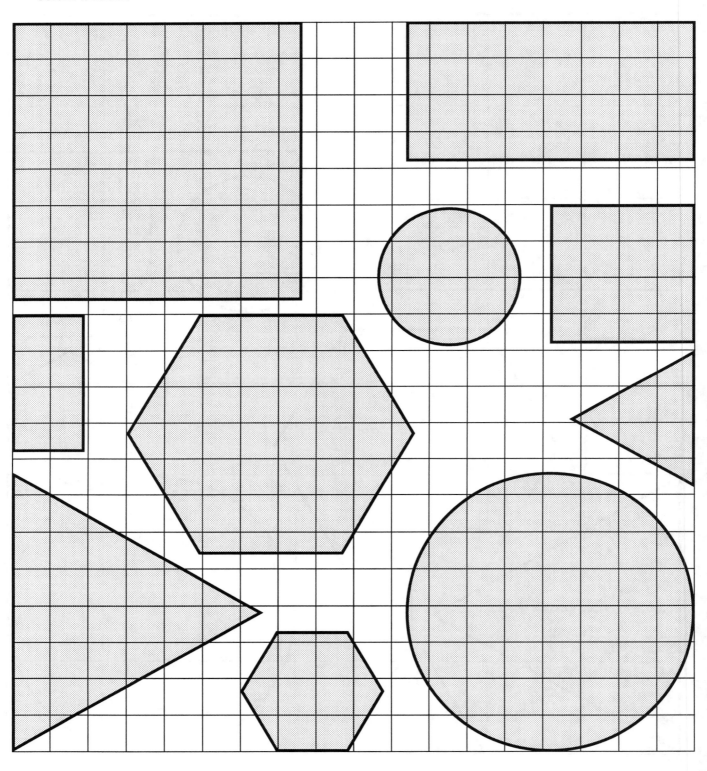

Solutions

Section A:
Learning About Shapes

Pages 10–14: Check children's tracing and coloring on the worksheets.

Section B: Shape Puzzles

Pages 17–22: Check children's tracing and coloring on the worksheets.

Page 23: At least 7 solutions

Number of Blocks	■	▪	▮	▪
1	1			
2			2	
3		2	1	
4		4		
4		1	1	2
5		3		2
6		2		4
7		1		6

Page 24:

Number of Blocks	⬡	⬢	▲	▲
3			3	
4	1		1	2
6			2	4
7	1			6

Page 25:

Number of Blocks	▲	▲	▮	▪	■
3	2		1		
4	2				2
5	2			2	1
6	2			4	
6	1	4	1		
7	1	4			2
8	1	4		2	1
9	1	4		4	

Section C:
More Shape Puzzles

Page 28: At least 22 solutions.

Number of Blocks	■	▪	▮	▪
4	1	1	2	
5	1	3	1	
5	1		2	2
5		1	4	
6	1	5		
6		3	3	
6			4	2
7	1	4		2
7		5	2	
7		2	3	2
8	1		3	4
8	1		1	6
8		4	2	2
8		1	3	4
9			3	6
9	1	2		6
9		6	1	2
9		3	2	4
10		2	2	6
10		5	1	4
11		4	1	6
12		6		6

Page 29: At least 40 solutions.

Number of Blocks	■	▪	▮	▪
4	4			
5	3	2		
6	2	4		
6	3	2	1	
7	3	1	1	2
7	3		4	
7	2	3	2	
7	1	6		
8	3		3	2
8	2	2	4	
8	3	1		4
8	2	3	1	2
8	1	5	2	
9	3		2	4
9	2	1	6	
9	1	4	4	
9	1	5	1	2

(continued)

Number of Blocks	■	▪	▌	▪
10	3		1	6
10	2	1	5	2
10	1	4	3	2
10	2	2	2	4
10	1	5		4
10		6	4	
11	2	1	4	4
11	2	2	1	6
11	1	4	2	4
11		5	6	
12	2	1	3	6
12		6	2	4
12	1	4	1	6
12	1	3	4	4
12		5	5	2
13	2		5	6
13		6	1	6
13		5	4	4
13	1	3	3	6
14	1	2	5	6
14		4	6	4
14		5	3	6
15		4	5	6

M: At least 21 solutions.

Number of Blocks	■	▌	▪	▪
2	2			
3	1		2	
4	1	2	1	
4			4	
5	1	4		
5		2	3	
5	1	1	1	2
6		4	2	
6	1	3		2
6	1		1	4
6	1	3		2
6		1	3	2
7		3	2	2
7			3	4
7	1	2		4
8	1	1		6
8		2	2	4
9		1	2	6
10		3	1	6
10		6		4
11		5		6

Page 30:

G: 1 small rectangle

H: 1 small square and 1 small rectangle; 3 small rectangles

J: 2 small squares; 4 small rectangles; 1 small square and 2 small rectangles

K:

Number of Blocks	▌	▪	▪
2	1		1
3		2	1
4		1	3
5			5

L:

Number of Blocks	▌	▪	▪
3	1		2
4		2	2
5		1	4
6			6

Page 31:

R: 1 small triangle

S: 1 large triangle; 4 small triangles

T: 1 large triangle and 5 small triangles; 1 large hexagon and 3 small triangles

U: 4 large triangles; 3 large triangles and 4 small triangles; 2 large triangles, 2 small triangles and 1 large hexagon; 1 large triangle, 6 small triangles, and 1 large hexagon

Page 32:

P: 2 large triangles; 1 large triangle and 4 small triangles; 1 large hexagon and 2 small triangles

Q: 2 small triangles

R: 4 small triangles

L: 4 large triangles; 2 large hexagons and 4 small triangles; 3 large triangles and 4 small triangles

Page 33:

A: 1 large hexagon and 1 small triangle; 1 large triangle and 3 small triangles

B: 1 small square and 1 small triangle; 2 small rectangles and 1 small triangle

Relational Attribute Blocks
© 1993 Learning Resources, Inc.

C: 1 small rectangle and 1 small triangle

D: At least 19 solutions.

Number of Blocks	■	▪	▲	▴	▮	▫
2	1		1			
3			1		2	
4		2	1		1	
5		4	1			
5		1	1		1	2
5	1			4		
6				4	2	
6		3	1			2
6		1			1	4
7		2	1			4
7		2		4	1	
8		4		4		
8		1	1			6
8		1		4	1	2
9		3		4		2
9				4	1	4
10		2		4		4
11		1		4		6

E: At least 8 solutions.

Number of Blocks	■	▪	▲	▴	▮	▫
2			1		1	
3		2	1			
5			1			4
5				4	1	
6		2	4			
7		1	4			2
8				4		4

Page 34:

A: 1 small rectangle and 2 small triangles

B: 2 small triangles, 1 small square and
1 small rectangle; 2 small triangles and
3 small rectangles

-**C:**

Number of Blocks	▮	▪	▲	▫
3	1		2	
4		2	2	
5		1	2	2
6			2	4

D: 2 large triangles and 2 small rectangles;
1 large triangle, 4 small triangles and
2 small rectangles

Page 35:

A: 1 large triangle and 4 small triangles;
1 large hexagon and 2 small triangles

B: 3 large triangles and 4 small triangles;
2 large hexagons and 4 small triangles;
1 large triangle, 1 large hexagon and
6 small triangles

Section D: Attribute Differences

Page 45: Sample answer

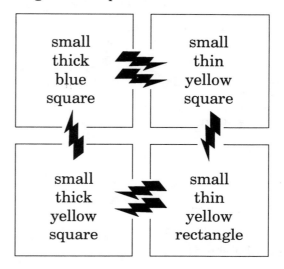

Page 46: Sample answer

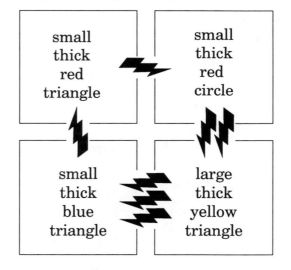

Section E: Logic Problems

Pages 49-51:

Set 1: large thick and thin red blocks

Set 2: thin red, yellow, and blue circles

Set 3: small thick blue squares and rectangles

Set 4: thin yellow hexagons

Set 5: all blocks except squares and rectangles

Set 6: all blocks except thin blue blocks

Set 7: large thick yellow and blue circles

Set 8: large and small thick red squares, rectangles, hexagons, and circles

Set 9: all large rectangles

Set 10: large thin red, yellow, and blue circles

Set 11: large red triangles, squares, and hexagons

Set 12: no blocks

Pages 52-54:

A: large thin blue circle

B: small thick yellow triangle

C: small thick red hexagon

D: large thin blue square

E: small thick red hexagon (or circle)

F: large thick yellow rectangle

G: large thick yellow circle

H: small thin blue circle

J: small thick blue circle

K: large thin yellow rectangle

L: small thin yellow hexagon

M: small thick blue rectangle (or square)

Section F: Making Arrangements

Page 57:

2-color circle on square

red-blue

yellow-blue

red-yellow

blue-yellow

blue-red

yellow-red

Page 58:

2-color hexagon on circle

red-blue

yellow-blue

red-yellow

blue-yellow

blue-red

yellow-red

Page 59:

3-color hexagon on circle on square

red-yellow-blue

yellow-red-blue

red-blue-yellow

blue-red-yellow

blue-yellow-red

yellow-blue-red

2-color: hexagon on circle on square

red-yellow-red

red-blue-red

yellow-red-yellow

yellow-blue-yellow

blue-red-blue

blue-yellow-blue

There are 12 other 2-color permutations when the same color blocks are next to each other.

Relational Attribute Blocks
© 1993 Learning Resources, Inc.

Page 60:

3-color circle and circle on rectangle

red-blue-yellow

blue-red-yellow

red-yellow-blue

yellow-red-blue

blue-yellow-red

yellow-blue-red

2-color circle and circle on rectangle

yellow-yellow-blue

yellow-yellow-red

red-red-yellow

red-red-blue

blue-blue-yellow

blue-blue-red

Page 61:

For each case, the 2- and 3-color permutations are the same as for page 59: circle on hexagon on rectangle, or hexagon on circle on rectangle.

Page 62:

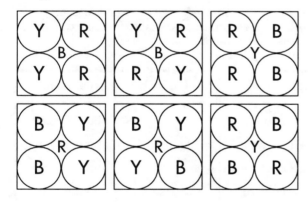

Page 63:

Here are the 2 different 3-color "styles." Since these hexagons are equilateral, rotating the shape may repeat a permutation.

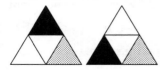

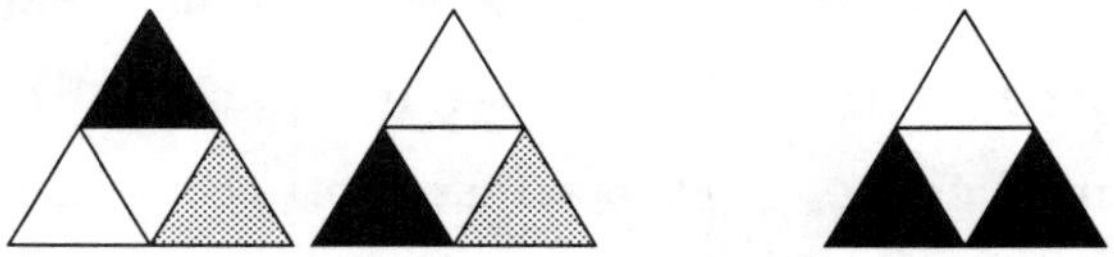

2-color "Style"

Page 64:

Here are three "styles." Since these hexagons are equilateral, rotating the shape may repeat a permutation.

Page 65: There are many solutions.

Section G: Shapes and Fractions

Page 68:

1. ½   2. ½   3. ½   4. ½

Page 69:

1. ¼   2. ¾   3. ¼   4. ¼

Page 70:

1. ⅙   2. ⅚   3. ³⁄₆ (or ½)   4. ²⁄₆ (or ⅓)

Page 71:

1. small blue square, small red square

2. small blue square, small red square, small yellow square

3. 2 small yellow rectangles, 2 small red rectangles

4. 2 small red triangles, 1 small blue triangle, 1 small yellow triangle

Page 72:

1. large blue rectangle, small blue square, small red square

2. small red square, small red rectangle, 2 small blue rectangles, 1 small yellow rectangle

3. large red rectangle and small red square, large yellow rectangle and small yellow square, large blue rectangle and small blue square

1.

Number of Blocks			
3	1R	1B, 1Y	
4	1R	1Y	2B
4	1R	1B	2Y
5	1R		2B, 2Y
4		2R, 1B, 1Y	
5		2R, 1B	2Y
5		2R, 1Y	2B
5		1R, 1B, 1Y	2R
6		2R	2Y, 2B

2. 2 small blue triangles, 2 small yellow triangles and 2 small red triangles

3.

Number of Blocks				
3	1B	1B, 1R		
4	1B	1B	2R	
4	1B	1R	2B	
5	1B	1B	1R	2R
5	1B	1R	1B	2B
5		2B, 1R	2B	
6	1B		2B, 1R	2R
6	1B		1B, 2R	2B
6		2B	2B, 2R	
7	1B		1B, 1R	2B, 2R
7		2B	2B, 1R	2R
7		2B	1B, 2R	2B
8		2B	1B, 1R	2B, 2R

Page 74: Sample answers are shown here There may be more solutions.

1.

2. 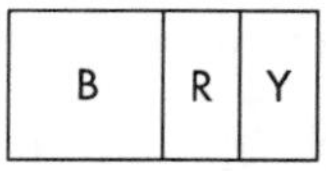 **3.** 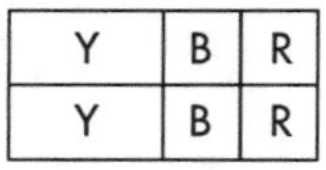 **4.**

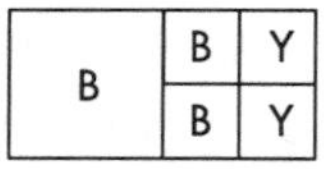

Page 75: Sample answers are shown here. There may be more solutions.

1. 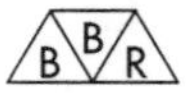 **2.** 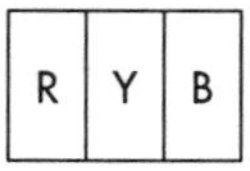 **3.** 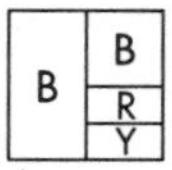 **4.**

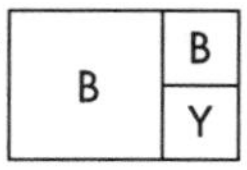

Section H: Perimeter and Area

Page 79:

    Square: P = 8 units
    Triangle: P = 6 units
    Hexagon: P = 6 units
    Circle: C = about 6 units
    Rectangle: P = 6 units

Page 80:

    Large triangle: P = 12 units
    Small triangle: P = 6 units
    Large hexagon: P = 12 units
    Small rectangle: P = 6 units
    Large square: P = 16 units
    Small square: P = 8 units
    Large circle: C = about 12 units

Page 81: Refer to the chart on page 94.

Page 82: Refer to the charton page 94.

Page 83:   **A:** 4   **B:** 2   **C:** 4   **D:** 2½

Page 84:   **A:** 2   **B:** 4   **C:** 3   **D:** 6   **E:** 7

Pages 85-86: Estimated area using counting; children's estimates will vary. For more precise area measurements, refer to the chart on page 94.

Block	Area in inches	Area in cm
large square	9 sq. in.	about 56 cm²
small square	2¼ sq. in.	about 14 cm²
large rectangle	4½ sq. in.	about 30 cm²
small rectangle	about 1 sq. in.	about 8 cm²
large triangle	about 4 sq. in.	about 25 cm²
small triangle	about 1 sq. in.	about 6-7 cm²
large hexagon	about 6 sq. in.	about 38 cm²
small hexagon	about 1½ sq. in.	about 9 cm²
large circle	about 7 sq. in.	about 45 cm²
small circle	about 1½ sq. in.	about 11 cm²

Relational Attribute Block Relationships

■ Square
All four sides are equal in length.
All angles are right angles (90°).
Four small squares can cover one large square.
The side of a large square is twice as long as the side of the small square.

▬ Rectangle
Pairs of opposite sides are equal in length.
All four angles are right angles (90°).
Four small rectangles can cover one large rectangle.
The longer side of each rectangle is twice as long as its shorter side.

■ Square and ▬ Rectangle
Two large rectangles can cover one large square.
Two small rectangles can cover one small square.
Two small squares can cover one large rectangle.
The side of a large square is the same length as the longer side of a large rectangle.
The side of a small square is the same length as the shorter side of a large rectangle.
The side of a small square is the same length as the longer side of a small rectangle.

▲ Triangle
The triangles are equilateral; all three sides are equal.
The three angles are equal (60° each).
Four small triangles can cover one large triangle.
The side of a large triangle is twice as long as the side of a small triangle.

■ Square, ▬ Rectangle, ▲ and Triangle
The side of a large square is the same length as the side of a large triangle.
The side of a small square is the same length as the side of a small triangle.
The side of a large triangle is the same length as the longer side of a large rectangle.
The side of a small triangle is the same length as the shorter side of a large rectangle.
The side of a small triangle is the same length as the longer side of a small rectangle.

⬡ Hexagon
The hexagons are regular hexagons (with equal sides and equal angles.
Each angle is twice as large as the angles in the triangles (120° each).

▬ Rectangle and ⬡ Hexagon
The side of a large hexagon is the same length as the shorter side of a large rectangle.
The side of a large hexagon is the same length as the longer side of a small rectangle.
The side of a small hexagon is the same length as the shorter side of a small rectangle.

■ Square and ⬡ Hexagon
The side of a small square is as long as the side of a large hexagon.

▲ Triangle and ⬡ Hexagon
Six small triangles can cover one large hexagon.
The side of a small triangle is as long as the side of a large hexagon.

● Circle
The diameter of a large circle is twice as long as the diameter of a small circle.

● Circle and ■ Square
The large circle can be inscribed in the large square so that the sides of the circle are tangent to the sides of the square.
The small circle can be inscribed in the small square so that the sides of the circle are tangent to the sides of the square.

● Circle and ⬡ Hexagon
The large hexagon can be inscribed in the large circle.
The small hexagon can be inscribed in the small circle.

Relational Attribute Block Dimensions

Dimensions in Inches

Shape		Size	Dimensions	Perimeter	Area
Square	■	large	3" per side	P = 12"	A = 9 sq. in.
	■	small	1½" each side	P = 6"	A = 2¼ sq. in.
				(P = 4s)	(A = s²)
Rectangle	▬	large	3" by 1½"	P = 9"	A = 4½ sq. in.
	▬	small	1½" by ¾"	P = 4½"	A = 1⅛ sq. in.
				(P = 2l + 2w)	(A = lw)
Triangle	▲	large	3" per side	P = 9"	A = 3 ¹⁵⁄₁₆ sq. in.
			(h = 2⅝")		or 3.9375 sq. in.
	▲	small	1½" per side	P = 4½"	A = ⁶³⁄₆₄ sq. in.
			(h = 1⁵⁄₁₆")		or 0.984375 sq. in.
				(P = 3s)	(A = ½ bh)
Hexagon	⬢	large	1½" per side	P = 9"	A = 5²⁹⁄₃₂ sq. in.
					or 5.90625 sq. in.
	⬢	small	¾" per side	P = 4½"	A = 1⁶¹⁄₁₂₈ sq. in.
			(h = ²¹⁄₃₂")		or 1.4765625 sq. in.
				(P = 6s)	(A = 6 triangles)
Circle	●	large	3" diameter	C = 9.42"	A = 7.065 sq. in.
	●	small	1½" diameter	C = 4.71"	A = 1.766 sq. in.
			(π = 3.14)	(C = πd)	(A = πr²)

Note: The height (h) of each triangle is approximate and was determined using the Pythagorean Thereom.

Dimensions in Centimeters

Shape		Size	Dimensions	Perimeter	Area
Square	■	large	7.5 cm per side	P = 30 cm	A = 56.25 cm²
	■	small	3.75 cm each side	P = 15 cm	A = 14.06 cm²
				(P = 4s)	(A = s²)
Rectangle	▬	large	7.5 by 3.75 cm	P = 22.5 cm	A = 28.13 cm²
	▬	small	3.75 by 1.875 cm	P = 11.25 cm	A = 7.05 cm²
				(P = 2l + 2w)	(A = lw)
Triangle	▲	large	7.5 cm per side	P = 22.5 cm	A = 24.64 cm²
			(h = 6.56 cm)		
	▲	small	3.75 cm per side	P = 11.25 cm	A = 6.15 cm²
			(h = 3.28 cm)	(P = 3s)	(A = 0.5bh)
Hexagon	⬢	large	3.75 cm per side	P = 22.5 cm	A = 36.9 cm²
	⬢	small	1.875 cm per side	P = 11.25 cm	A = 9.25 cm²
			(h = 1.64 cm)	(P = 6s)	(A = 6 triangles)
Circle	●	large	7.5 cm diameter	C = 23.55 cm	A = 44.16 cm²
			(3.75 cm radius)		
	●	small	3.75 cm diameter	C = 11.78 cm	A = 11.04 cm²
			(1.875 cm radius)		
			(π = 3.14)	(C = πd)	(A = πr²)

Note: One inch is approximately 2.5 centimeters. The dimensions 3.75 and 1.875 were determined by halving 7.5 twice; actual measurements may vary and may be rounded to the nearest tenth (3.8 cm and 1.9 cm). In the metric system, the area "square centimeters" is usually expressed as "cm²" rather than "sq. cm."

Family-Gram

Dear Family,

_____

_____

_____

_____

_____ Date   Teacher _____

Good Work
Certificate

TO: _____

FOR: _____

_____ Date   Teacher _____

Relational Attribute Blocks

Award

TO: _____

FOR: _____

_____

_____

_____

_____
Date   Teacher